GROWING SEASONS FOR LITTLE CHARACTERS

GROWING SEASONS

SEASONS for LITTLE CHARACTERS

REBECCA BERTOLINI

VICTOR BOOKS

A DIVISION OF SCRIPTURE PRESS PUBLICATIONS INC.
USA CANADA ENGLAND

**Dedicated to Dad and Mom who
are such good parents to me.**

Scripture quotations in this book are from the New
American Standard Bible, © the Lockman Foundation
1960, 1962, 1963, 1968, 1971, 1973, 1975, 1977.
Other quotations are from The Living Bible, © 1971,
Tyndale House Publishers, Wheaton, IL 60189.
Used by permission.

Copyediting: Afton Rorvik
Cover Design: Grace K. Chan Mallette
Cover Photo: Uniphoto/Jim Whitmer
Interior Illustrations: Marilee Harrold-Pilz/
Becky Radtke/Bron Smith/Joe Van Severen

CONTENTS

Jul.	2	sea creatures	deep/shallow	118
Jul.	3	rules	right/wrong	120
Jul.	4	directions	left/right	121
Aug.	1	ecology	dirty/clean	129
Aug.	2	safety	safe/dangerous	130
Aug.	3	manners	loud/soft	131
Aug.	4	habits	beginning/end	133

SEASON: AUTUMN   THEME: JOY AND THANKFULNESS

Month	Week	Unit Study	Concept Words	
Sep.	1	first aid	moving/still	145
Sep.	2	music	stop/go	146
Sep.	3	senses	soft/hard	147
Sep.	4	caregivers	strong/weak	149
Oct.	1	physics	forward/backward	157
Oct.	2	money	lost/found	158
Oct.	3	holidays	before/after	160
Oct.	4	plants	alive/not alive	161
Nov.	1	future	light/dark	167
Nov.	2	shapes	over/under	168
Nov.	3	history	sequences	169
Nov.	4	discipline	bright/dull	170

INTRODUCTION

My four-year-old daughter Ashley and I were praying in bed the night before we were to take off in an airplane for Cincinnati. After the usual requests, she concluded her petition with the words, "And help us not to fall out of the windows of the plane. In Jesus' name, Amen." I have learned that during our evening devotions, my children's deepest emotions and most sacred ideals often surface. I listen very carefully for clues that will reveal cherished hopes, innermost feelings, and personal resolve so that I might become a part of the molding process.

That night the issue to be dealt with was clearly visible. But other times it is necessary for me to dig and pry in order to figure out the actual concern. I remember when my son David was still a little boy. He asked, "Mom, is God bigger than an elephant?" After receiving my affirmative reply, he continued, "Is He bigger than our house? Is He bigger than the park? Is He bigger than the whole world?" I nodded after each and every query, but then the questioning stopped. Sensing by the puzzled expression still creasing his face that we had not yet uncovered the origin of all the confusion, I prodded further for a probable cause. Finally , I uncovered the worry underlying the verbalized questions. "If God is that big," he asked, "how can He fit in my heart?" Not a bad theological query for a preschooler to be pondering, eh?

These are the types of teachable moments we try to create in this book. We introduce games, songs, stories, finger plays, and activities with the purpose of encouraging growth in a knowledge of God and His ways. However, when these pliable moments occur on their own, we should do everything we can to keep them from slipping through our fingers. Think of the tremendous potential that my children's unassuming, but vitally significant, revelations offered to me as a parent. Ashley's fear freed me to introduce God's omnipotence, and David's concern gave me the perfect chance to present God's omnipresence. How can we make the most of these unexpected chances to teach? How can we maximize the less subtle, but still fleeting, times that we have set aside for that purpose?

First, we start with a plan. If we want to promote the character qualities that are so important to us, we must determine our direction and work toward achievement. This book provides a program with which we can work. It is divided into four sections, one for each season of the year. The chapters are prefaced with brief introductions discussing our goals and roles as parents and how to correct and direct our children. The activities themselves are divided into the following sets of character building studies:

Winter—love/giving
Spring—patience/discernment
Summer—obedience/responsibility
Fall—joy/thanksgiving

This arrangement allows three full months of repetition and reinforcement on each theme in order for the twin virtues to thoroughly permeate our preschoolers' lives. The individual weeks themselves begin with a Bible or character story presenting an aspect of the seasonal theme. The other activities (including academics, word concepts, and mini units about our world), derive their ideas and substance from the Bible story which launched the week. Presenting the same focus in five different ways (one for each day of the workweek), will help to solidify that particular facet in your child's heart and mind before moving on to another topic.

The following symbols will help you to determine the project within the week that is best suited for the particular moment you have on hand.

You don't have to have a doctorate in childhood education to teach character to your children. You don't have to be a skilled storyteller on the level of a Hans Christian Andersen in order to make the lessons come alive. The only ingredients you will need to make this book work for you are a heart of love and a sincere desire to develop within your child the virtues that count. As far as the supplementary materials to pull off these activities, the projects require no other paraphernalia than an ordinary household would be able to supply.

Despite our lofty aspirations and deliberate preparations, however, nothing is ever predictable, especially when dealing with children. You never know what they will do or how they will respond. I remember one particular Sunday in children's church. I held up a clear glass of water as a visual illustration to represent our lives before we sin. Then I mixed in a spoonful of dirt. Only a spoonful, but it permeated the whole glass just the way a small sin will infiltrate every part of our lives. The glass looked putrid as the soil swirled around the edges and started to settle at the bottom. Confident that my illustration was well understood and applied, I asked how many children would now be willing to take a big gulp of water from the glass. I was shocked when ten hands immediately shot up. Evidently, I had a class full of daredevils, but I could never drive the point home as long as they viewed the glass clean enough for drinking water. Receiving a sudden surge of inspiration, I told them I had left out an important piece of information. The dirt had been taken from my cat's litter box. The hands were instantly withdrawn. With a sigh of relief, I relaxed. The illustration was saved. Until my son, who sat in the very center of the class, piped up to say, "But, Mom, we don't even have a cat!"

Not only are children unpredictable, but so is everything else in life. Another Sunday morning in church, my friend was leading the class while I assisted. Her illustration involved a glass as well. It looked empty, but unbeknownst to the children, there was a transparent layer of bleach in the bottom. Setting it squarely in the middle of a table, she held up another glass for all the little ones to see. This one was filled with an ominously dark liquid.

Confidently, she explained to her breathless audience what she was about to do. "I will take the glass I am holding, black with sin, and pour it into the empty glass to show what the Lord Jesus can do in our lives." Because we had actually tried this experiment earlier in the week, we knew that the bleach would counteract the food coloring and the liquid would instantaneously become as clear as crystal. Then she could talk about Christ's perfect and complete forgiveness. But this time (perhaps we had put in too much food coloring or not enough bleach) the color changed but did not disappear. What could a teacher do with an illustration like that? Say that Jesus' blood washes away only part of our sin?

I had already shifted into panic gear and was ready to scrap the whole thing and move on with the next activity. But not my friend. She was the master of the moment. "Look, children!" she said with excitement, holding high the glass of peachy colored liquid. "Remember how ugly the water was before Jesus took care of our sin? Well, look at the lovely color it turned into. The Lord always makes something beautiful out of our lives!"

This illustration demonstrates exactly what we want to attempt in this book. We conceive, strategize, and work toward building into the lives of our children an understanding of biblical truth and an accompanying lifestyle. But we don't have to be discouraged by the inevitable interruption or unexpected twist of our child's focus. We can incorporate it into part of the lesson and use it to enhance our original plan. Don't be thrown off guard when your child comes up with an unanticipated reply or a disconcerting question. These are the openings we should most cherish and seize as prime occasions for instruction. These are the opportunities that could never be duplicated for all the scheming and contriving in the world.

WINTER THEME: love and giving

INTRODUCTION

We were on our way to the mountains. Settling into the front seat of the car, I let my worries blow out the window as we zipped onto the highway. I smiled in anticipation of the great time we would have together as a family. It would be the perfect day — blue skies, powdery snowdrifts, majestic trees, and towering cliffs.

Suddenly a bloodcurdling shriek shattered my idyllic dream. Convinced that nothing short of a python under the seat or a masked murderer behind the toboggan could evoke a scream of that magnitude from the throat of my daughter, I practically swerved into another car in my haste to pull to the side of the road. My heart trembled as I looked into the backseat. What would I find?

Ashley's arms were folded and her lips fixed into a pout. "David put his elbow on my side of the car!" she accused, sticking out her tongue at her brother.

Quick to defend, David shoved and shouted, "Did not!" Breaking into the impending argument, I attempted to bring peace by reminding them of the delightful time we were anticipating in the mountains. Only temporarily deterred, we had barely turned back onto the highway when the bickering continued in other forms. Ashley was singing too loud. David wouldn't tie Ashley's shoe. Ashley didn't share her pencil. David called Ashley stupid. Ad infinitum. We were only halfway to the lake, in the middle of some godforsaken wilderness, and I was ready to abandon them by the roadside with a sign for the next car passing by, "Take us, please!"

"OK," I hissed through clenched teeth, "the next person to speak will be in BIG trouble!" (I couldn't think of a formidable enough punishment to threaten them with on the spur of the moment.) "I don't want to hear any more out of you two for the rest of the trip."

"But Mom," Ashley said in a tremulous voice, "I have to go to the bathroom really bad."

Who was it who said children are the heritage of the Lord and that the fruit of the womb was a reward? (Ps. 127:3) What could that man have been thinking when he uttered, "Happy is the one with a quiver full" (Ps. 127:5). I couldn't even handle two of them on this one afternoon.

The joy of having children cannot be founded on their lovableness alone, for mortal creatures will not always be cute. It cannot be based on their performance alone, for immature creatures will not always be perfect. And it cannot be fueled by their displays of affection alone, for depraved creatures will not always act unselfishly.

But like God's nurturing love for us, His adopted children, there is tremendous fulfillment in succoring the dependent and defenseless. Doesn't it make your heart beat valiantly to be the champion of an admiring little boy or girl? Our children need heroes! (See Heb. 11:32-38.) Isn't there a joy in watching your offspring's attempts at imitation, knowing they are striving as hard as they can to be just like you? Let's be ready. (See 1 Cor. 11:1.) Isn't there profound pleasure in identifying and satisfying concrete needs in the lives of our children? What spiritual yearnings can we meet alongside the physical necessities? (See Matt. 7:9-11.)

Also following the example of our Father-God, we can delight in visualizing shining potential for purposeless, shapeless lives. Like an artist conceiving the perfect sculpture, we chip and sand (unhurriedly and deliberately) until corner by corner, line by line, we produce a showpiece that brings pleasure and delight. (See Heb. 12:6-11.) We should not try to live out in the lives of our young people all the fantasies and dreams of success that we could never fulfill when we were their age, but in the area of character and Christlikeness, we should strive to spur them on to excellence. (See Dan. 6:3-4.)

But great masterpieces do not happen inadvertently. The artist must have design and intent. He must work with a purpose behind every stroke. A reason for every line. As parents, we would be crazy to begin without a draft, a mold, or even an outline. What is it we want to accomplish? What are our goals for our children? What can we do to achieve these ideals? How do we spend the majority of our time and effort on what is most important? Can we bring our children daily before the Lord in prayer?

From several parental prayers recorded in the Bible, we can formulate a good list of aims and ambitions suitable for our own children. The following noteworthy requests are found in Genesis 17:18, 1 Chronicles 29:19, Job 1:5, and Matthew 17:15. We desire:

- that our children would be raised with a God-consciousness.
- that they would have a heart for God and a desire to know Him intimately.
- that they would keep God's laws.
- that they would please God in their service.
- that their sins would be forgiven.
- that they would experience God's mercy.

We cannot know what circumstances and situations will have the most impact on our children in the years to come. We do not know what the future holds for our country, our physical health, our familial stability, or our children's educational options. Actually, all we have to work with is today. Consider the boy Daniel and his fearlessness to stand alone for what he believed to be right. And young Queen Esther, who put her own life on the line when the lives of her people were at stake. And Naaman's little servant girl, whose faith inspired a celebrated army captain to call on God. And Moses, who in his youth turned his back on the splendors of wealth and position to be counted with God's people. And the child Samuel, whose immediate obedience allowed God the freedom to speak and be heard. And Joseph, the son of Jacob, who credited God for incredible wisdom that most would have claimed for themselves.

The astounding thing about the parents of every single one of these young men and women was that they had only a few precious years to instill within the hearts of their children the characteristics that would affect the rest of their lives. Each one of these parents faced the devastation of separation from their son or daughter while the child was very young. The preschool years of a child's life are of ultimate importance in the establishment of lifelong patterns. And because these parents' goals were firmly established from the very beginning, the moments they did spend with their children were of the highest quality.

Are the virtues that characterized the young people in the previous paragraphs the same ones that we want to implant in our own children? If so, we must live, breathe, and eat them. What consumes us will also consume our children. The Bible says, "like people, like priest" (Hosea 4:9). This means that our kids don't even have a chance to excel beyond our own level of spirituality. The more that godliness becomes an established part of our own lifestyle, the easier it will pass on. Children love to play "Simon Says" and "Follow the Leader." Why? Because children are the greatest imitators in the world. Now they are looking to us.

After the principles most important to us have been made an integral part of our own lifestyle, we seek to teach these characteristics in any way we can. We read our children stories that will impart a desire for living according to godly principles. We look for these principles as they are displayed in nature. We do projects that require their outworking. We memorize verses that speak of them. We do activities that encourage and promote them. We sing songs that refer to them. We point out people who have learned to live them. We incorporate, enhance, and establish them into habits and patterns. And then when our children are older, they will not depart from them.

DECEMBER
WEEK ONE

BEST BUDDIES

story   object lesson

Objective: to show that love and sharing go hand in hand.

Materials needed: a bathrobe, belt, knife (dull blade), and a stick (to represent an arrow).

Put on the robe and belt. Stash the knife in a pocket and slide the stick through your belt. Tell the following story of Jonathan and David from 1 Samuel 18. When you get to the part about Jonathan sharing his robe, belt, knife, and arrows, remove each item and hand it to your child as a visual example of giving.

David was going to be the next king of Israel. Saul, the man who was now the king, hated David for that. Saul wanted his own son Jonathan to be the next king. Jonathan could have hated David too. But he didn't. As a matter of fact, David and Jonathan were best friends. It didn't matter to Jonathan that David was going to take his place. He loved David with all his heart.

It all started when David killed the mighty giant Goliath. David told King Saul all about how the tiny stone struck the huge giant in the forehead so squarely that he fell with a might thud to the earth. Jonathan listened to the story breathlessly. From that moment on, he knew he wanted to friends with David.

When David moved to the palace, he and Jonathan probably did lots of fun things together. You can imagine that they went hunting, swimming, hiking, and fishing. I'm sure they spent quiet times together too when they would just sit and talk. Jonathan was always trying to share. One time he took off his princely robe and a special belt that he wore and gave them to David. He also gave him a shiny knife and an excellent set of bow and arrows. You can be sure they were the best in the land. But when you love someone, you can't help but share with them the nicest things that you have.

Soon Jonathan's father started to hate David. He even tried to kill him. David had to run away and Jonathan helped him escape. The two friend hugged and cried for a long time. They would really miss each other. But even though they could not be together, they would continue to be friends for the rest of their lives.

FRIENDSHIP FRUIT

object lesson

Objective: to stimulate your child to become the best possible friend with many admirable qualities.

Materials needed: 2 baskets or bowls, 10 pieces of fruit, and 10 strips of masking tape.

Label nine pieces of fruit, using the strips of masking tape, with the spiritual qualities found in Galatians 5:22 — love, joy, peace, patience, kindness, goodness, faithfulness, gentleness, and self-control. Put them into one basket. Pick one of the same virtues to label the piece of fruit that remains and put it in the other basket. With your child, think about how each of these fruits would enhance any relationship. For example, patience would mean waiting your turn in a game, and gentleness would mean treating your friends' toys with care. Pretend each basket represents a person. Which one would your child pick to be his best friend? The basket with lots of fruit or the basket with only one? Which basket would your child want to represent himself? Would he have more friends if he had all those fruits in his life?

GIFTS OF LOVE

skill   word concepts

Objective: to demonstrate the difference between *giving* and *receiving*.
Materials needed: wrapping paper, ribbon, tape, scissors, and a small gift.

Let your child look through his own possessions for something he wants to wrap and then give to you. You can do the same thing for him with some small item like an eraser, balloon, or piece of gum. Let your child wrap the present he is giving, as independently as possible, encouraging creativity in packaging. Wrap your surprise and present the gifts to each other with clarification on who is *giving* and who is *receiving*.

HERBAL WREATH

pre- reading   arts/ crafts

Objective: to give opportunity to practice letter writing and to make a cheerful card to give away.
Materials needed: construction paper, markers, glue, a bowl, and various good-smelling and interesting-looking spices.

Fold a piece of construction paper in half. Trace a circle on the front using a small bowl as a guide. Glue cloves, allspice, cinnamon, and other pungent herbs around the ring to form a wreath. On the inside, let the child write as many letters of a greeting as he can. While you work together, talk about the Bible story of the week and how loving means giving. Decide who should receive this card.

BIRD FEEDER

nature science   arts/ crafts   physical activity

Objective: to further the mind-set of giving to the less fortunate.
Materials needed: pine cone, string, peanut butter, birdseed, and a knife.

Tie a string to the stem of a pine cone. Spread peanut butter on the surface of the pine cone and sprinkle liberally with bird seed. Discuss while working on this project how difficult it is for birds to find food in the winter. Who else could use our help this time of year? Hang the feeder in a tree, observable from the windows of your house.

WEEK TWO

BOULDER BREAKING

object lesson   story   nature science   word concepts

Objective: to see that sharing requires not only giving away what belongs to you but also giving of yourself.
Materials needed: several rocks of various sizes.

First, have your child place the rocks in order from biggest to smallest. Then tell the following story, starting with the biggest rock and progressing until it has broken into little pebbles. Talk about what it means to give of yourself—letting others go first, taking a small piece of cake or playing a game with your friend that is not your favorite.

At the top of a huge mountain, the water from melting snows trickled into a tiny crack on the face of a huge rock. The water froze into ice and pushed at the crack until it was split far enough apart for you to get your hand inside. Finally, with a mighty splintering sound, a huge section of the rock gave way and went crashing down, down the steep cliffs. The big rock bounced crazily off the sides of the mountain. With each bounce the rock broke off little pieces of itself to make other smaller rocks. These also went flying faster and faster down to the valley below. A few got stuck on ledges here and there, but most found themselves in the bubbles of a tiny stream that gurgled and sputtered down the valley over lots of other little rocks just like themselves. Well, almost like themselves. As the new stones looked through the sparkling water at the others already resting peacefully on the sandy bottom, they could see that the longer a rock had been in the water, the smoother it looked. Their own edges were sharp and their sides were rough. But just as the giant mountain with its jagged peaks had given of itself to make the big rock that went crashing down its side, and just as the big rock had allowed itself to be broken apart to form the smaller rocks, so the smaller rocks would be broken over time by the rushing of the water until they became perfect pebbles. The little bits and pieces shaved off by the stream would make the soft, lovely sand at the river bottom. So even the little rocks would learn the joy of giving to others.

VOLCANIC ACTION

Objective: to illustrate the force and action of a volcano and to enhance the geological facts presented in the previous character story.
Materials needed: vinegar, baking powder, orange food coloring, and a transparent glass or jar.

Mix a few drops of food coloring with the vinegar in a glass. Add the baking powder and watch the reaction. Compare it to the tremendous forces within the earth and what hot lava looks like when it breaks through the crust. Review the story of the breaking rock, and explain that many rocks are made out of hardened lava from the volcanic action of the earth.

STRONGER THAN ROCK

Objective: to illustrate *big* and *small* and give another miniature geology lesson.
Materials needed: small freezable container, masking tape, and water.

Plan an experiment to demonstrate that a *small* amount of water will get *bigger* when frozen. Use the tape to mark the halfway point on the outside of the container. Fill with water to that line. Put in the freezer. Come back later and see how the water has swollen over the line. Explain how water can flow into the crack of a rock, freeze, and eventually split the rock. Contrast the small crack in the story with the eventual big split.

MINERAL SETS

Objective: to differentiate between different numbered sets.
Materials needed: a pencil and the activity sheet (p. 21).

Follow the directions, matching and identifying the bigger and smaller sets within each section.

SAND LAYERING

Objective: to use two geological compounds (sodium and limestone) to create an attractive decoration.
Materials needed: a small transparent jar or bottle with a lid (like a baby food jar), colored chalk, and salt.

Grate, sand, or grind the chalk into powder. Make a separate pile for each color and mix with salt to add substance. As you handle the soft powder, remind your child of the eventual destiny of the big rock in the story— it was ground into sand. As you work together on the project, see if you can come up with ten different ways a child can give himself to others. Pour the colors into the bottle one on top of the other so that you can see each individual layer. Be careful not to bump the container or the colors will become mixed. Fill it as full as you can and close the lid tightly.

WEEK THREE

THE PERFECT GIFT

story   activity

Objective: to show that a gift doesn't have to be expensive and to demonstrate that the best gift is one that meets a need.

Tell the following story found in Acts 3. When you get to the part about the man's response to Peter's command, your child can imitate the man in the story. He can walk (lift legs up and down), leap (jump into the air), and praise the Lord (clap hands).

There once was a sad looking man sitting at the gate of the temple. He would hold out his arm and beg the people passing by to drop a few coins into the cup he clutched in his hand. He had been sitting in that same spot for many years because even as a little boy something was wrong with his legs. He had never walked a step in his life.

Peter and John were passing by and looked over at the ragged man. When the sad man saw them, he held out the cup in a hopeful way and asked if they would give him money. Peter didn't have a nickel or a dime in his pocket, but he knew he did have something that the man would like even more.

He spoke to the man and said, "I do not have any silver and I do not have any gold." The poor man's face probably fell and his outstretched arm drooped. Then Peter continued, "But what I do have I will gladly give you." In wonder the lame man looked up into Peter's kindly eyes. What could a man with no money do for him? "In the name of Jesus Christ," Peter declared, "get up and walk!"

Walk! That's what the man had always wanted to do! Could it be possible? Was the name of Jesus so powerful that weak little legs that had never supported a body before could suddenly stand and walk? He would try. He stretched out his legs and leaped up in the air. He was completely healed! More excited than he had ever been in his whole life, he ran in and out of the crowds gathered for worship in the temple. He jumped and frolicked and praised the wonderful name that had made him well. Jesus!

EXERCISE SONG

music   activity

Objective: to use all the parts of the body and to review the Bible story.
Materials needed: the activity sheet (p. 23).

Talk about what it would mean to be physically impaired like the man in the Bible story. Think of how wonderful it would feel to be miraculously healed. Enjoy the physical activity the song provides. The words are set to the tune of "London Bridge."

WHEN YOU'RE UP, YOU'RE UP

concepts   activity

Objective: to play off Peter's command and contrast *up* and *down*.

What did Peter ask the lame man to do? Walk around your house and let your child put *up* everything that can be made to go up — light switches, window shades, ironing boards, water in the bathtub, toy box lids, etc. Then retrace your steps and put them all *down*. Use the applicable word up or down with each item.

ROLLER COASTER LETTERS

Objective: to reinforce the sights and sounds of various alphabetical letters and review the concepts of up vs. down.

Materials needed: 10 to 26 index cards, crayons, and tape.

Before the lesson, write one alphabetical letter on each card. Make half of the letters on the cards upper case and the other half lower case. Prepare them to be stuck on the wall with tape when ready. First, however, place them on a flat surface for your child to look over. Call out a certain letter and instruct him to hang the corresponding card on the wall. If it is a capital letter, he should put it up on the wall, as high as he can reach. The lower case letters can be stuck down low on the wall. After the exercise, reflect together about how the crippled man could never have done this exercise until God healed him. Was Peter's gift better than money?

THE SQUEAKY WHEEL

Objective: to give by meeting a need.

Materials needed: can of oil.

Find a door, chair, wheel, or something else that needs to be oiled. Grease the noisy part until the offending sound is silenced. Discuss any needs you know of in your family, church, or community that ought to be met. Could you take a lunch to a family that is sick? Wash the walls of the church nursery? Whitewash graffiti off a city building?

HELPING THE HURTING

story

Objective: to encourage loving reactions to people who are suffering.

Within the context of family and friends, think of a recent time when your child hurt someone else, deliberately or inadvertently. Recall the incident to his mind and then tell the following story found in 2 Chronicles 28. After the narration, ask your child to think more about the personal illustration with which you began. How could he go back and help those he hurt?

When the nation of Israel loved God and did what He said, God watched over them. He made sure they had good crops, fat animals, and lots of happy, healthy children. But sometimes, God's people would forget about Him. They would steal, lie, murder, and do all the things God hates. When they did not act right as proper children of God, God had to discipline them, just as Dad and Mom must do if you disobey.

One time the Israelites became so evil it hurt God to watch them sin any more. So He sent rough soldiers to capture and burn their cities. The enemies cruelly dragged the people away from their homes.

But God was still Israel's Father. He loved and felt sorry for His people in their troubled times. He sent a messenger to talk to the enemy and ask them to be nice to the poor, suffering people. The enemies started to look on God's children with compassion. They found clothes to cover them. They gave the starving people some food. Those that were dying of thirst were given water. They fixed their wounds and put the sickest people on the backs of donkeys. Then they took them to a city near where they had lived so that relatives and friends could care for them.

In this story the enemies learned to see the nation of Israel through the eyes of God. Looking at people through the eyes of God means showing love and care.

VISITING A SENIOR

Objective: to overcome any obstacles in communicating with the elderly.

Dress up like an old person. Let your child carry on an imaginary visit with you. Show how an older person is one to whom we should show love and care. Demonstrate how to speak clearly and loudly. Have your child watch for ways to assist, like offering a chair or a helping hand when rising. Talk about how rowdy behavior might startle an older person. Discuss offering only foods that are easy to chew and digest. Plan a visit to an elderly relative or church member to try out what you have practiced. (See the next entry for a gift that you can take along.)

MAKING A CALL

Objective: to make a gift to take to the senior citizen you have arranged to visit.

Materials needed: two sheets of 8 1/2" x 11" construction paper, scissors, the activity sheet (p. 25) and clear contact paper (optional).

Follow the directions as specified. Talk about how pleasant it is to be giving things to other people that they can really use. Review proper decorum around the elderly.

THE RICHNESS OF THE POOR

Objective: to contrast *rich* and *poor* and to present the poor as a segment of society that we should care about.

Materials needed: two dolls or stuffed animals.

Set up house for one doll in a corner. Let her represent a *poor* family. Pretend she needs food, clothes, and furniture. Situate the other doll in another corner with all the trappings of a *rich* person. Let the rich doll happily share all of her material possessions with the poor doll. Pretend that the poor doll gratefully receives all the gifts. Then think of things the poor doll can share with the rich one — a bouquet of wildflowers, a cup of cold water, a friendly invitation to play, or a library book. Talk about how many elderly people with fixed incomes do not have a lot of material possessions, but still may have much to share. What other kinds of blessings may we receive from them?

ZOO VIEW

Objective: to think of things to enjoy with an older person and to do some exercises that relate to the letter z.

Materials needed: crayons and the activity sheet (p. 27).

Billy wants to see the lion. Follow the path from the zoo entrance to the lion's cage. What letter did your child write? What sound does the letter make? What letter does the word "zoo" start with? Ask your child to draw an animal that starts with the letter z, such as a zebra, next to the other animals. Going to the zoo is something a child could do wth a senior citizen. What are some other activities a child can enjoy with an elderly person?

(A) Match the things on the top with the bottom one to one.
(B) Circle the set with the same number of things.
(C) Which is the only precious stone that does not come from the ground?

1.

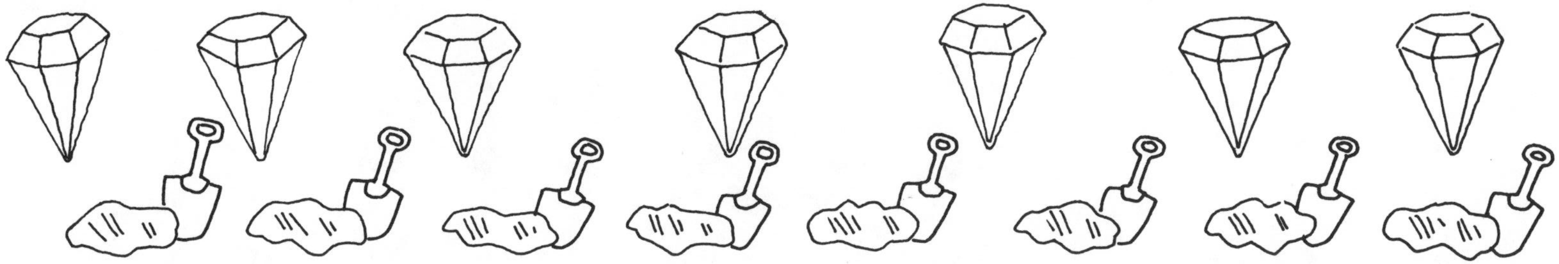

2.

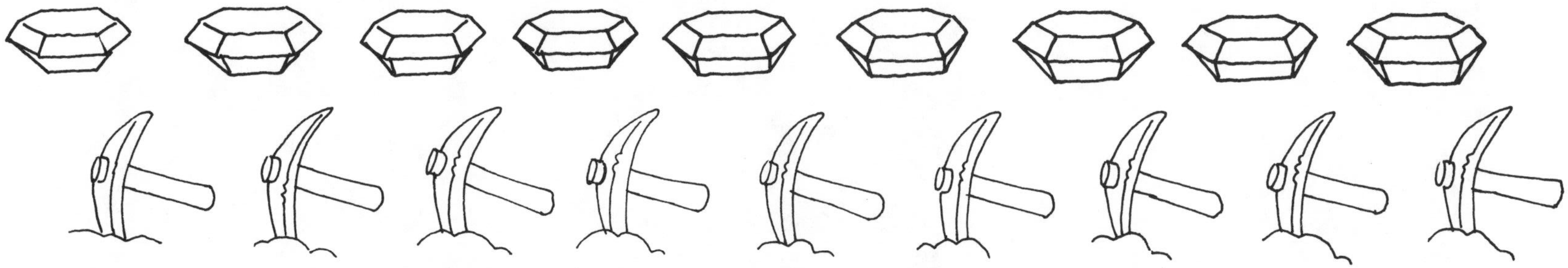

3.

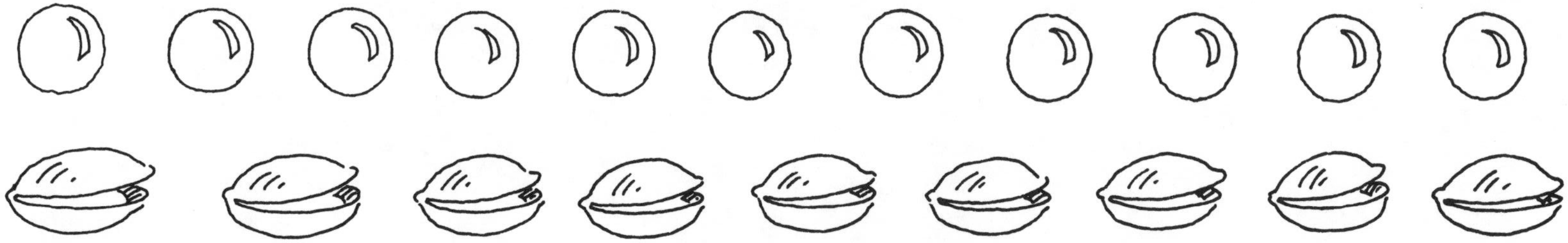

4.

(Touch each part of body mentioned.)

Head and shoul-ders   knees and toes

(Spread arms and turn.)

arms go out and   round you go

(Touch each part of body mentioned.)

Toes and shoul-ders   knees and head

(Lay on floor with hands for pillow.)

now lay down and   go to bed

1. Take a piece of construction paper and cut it into one inch lengthwise strips.

2. Fold another color construction paper in half lengthwise, cutting one inch strips going the other direction. This time stop an inch from the edge. Fold it open.

3. Weave each strip from the first sheet in and out of the second sheet.

4. Push each strip tightly against the others. After it is complete, you may wish to cover it with clear contact paper to keep it clean.

5. Make more if you wish and give them away to be used and enjoyed.

JANUARY
WEEK ONE

BIBLE MEMORY

pre- math   story   our world

Objective: to stir up a heart of compassion and love for children of other countries.

Count how many Bibles you have in your home. After presenting the story, think about what it would be like to live in another country where the Word of God is scarce and treasured.

"Are you coming?" Jorge stuck his head through the door and peered through the darkness into the corner of the room. Maria sat on her little cot crying.

"No," she mumbled through her tears. "Go on without me. I can't come today."

Jorge turned back into the brightness of the day. It just didn't make sense. Maria had been more excited than anyone about this day. The Bible teacher was to meet all the children down by the Orinoco River in Venezuela just as he did once every week. But this time, along with the songs and stories, he would give a Bible-book to anyone who had memorized twenty verses and could recite them without a mistake. Jorge wasn't even going to try. It sounded so impossible. But his friend Maria had spent hours poring over the sheet with the Bible verses. She stuck them on the walls of her house so she could see them as she did her chores. She practiced saying them to Jorge so many times he thought he was going to go crazy. "You have them perfect," he told her. "You don't need to say them anymore." But she kept at it anyway.

Jorge turned around and looked back into the doorway of the dingy little house. "Are you sure you don't want to come?" he asked. "This is the day to say all your verses!"

Maria just shook her head. "I have to watch my brothers and sisters while Mama goes to market. I guess I'll never get the Bible-book now."

Jorge shuffled his feet through the dust as he crossed through the village to get to the river. Poor Maria. She looked so sad. All of a sudden, he tightened his lips and straightened his shoulders. He would do anything to get a Bible-book for her. He had listened to Maria say the verses over and over, hadn't he? He ought to be able to remember the words. He would try.

Already many children were running down to the shore and gathering around the Bible teacher's boat. The man held up picture cards as he told them stories from the Bible. The children sang loudly when he led them in some choruses. Finally it was time to recite the verses. With a big lump in his throat, Jorge stepped forward. One by one the Scriptures that Maria had practiced came to his mind. Finally, he had only one left to say. But his mind was absolutely blank. Would he be able to bring a Bible-book to Maria after all?

Then he remembered that he could ask God for help. "Please let me think of the verse," he prayed silently in his head. In a moment, the last Scripture popped into his mind. Quickly, before he forgot it again, he blurted out the words.

"Good job," the Bible teacher said with a smile. "You must have worked very hard." Jorge smiled. He knew it was Maria who had worked so hard. And now she would be able to get the Bible-book she had wanted so badly.

MOM, I'M HUNGRY

our world   object lesson

Objective: to point out the advantages we enjoy because of where we live.

Materials needed: a bowl of rice.

For a meal, offer your child a simple bowl

of rice. Other than water to quench your child's thirst, do not give him anything else to eat except more rice. Even when your child asks for a snack, feed him only rice until the next meal. Use this deprivation of variety to illustrate the way children eat in many other lands. Emphasize that their portions may not even be as generous.

STRETCHING STRING

pre-math   word concepts   our world   physical activity

Objective: to create a visual contrast between *near* and *far*.

Materials needed: five objects and a length of string.

Place around the room the five items you have picked. Put some objects close to your child and some farther away. Ask him to state which are *near* and which are *far*. Use the string to determine questionable distances. Talk about the people you know. Which one lives nearest? Which one lives the farthest away? Do they live as far away as Jorge and Maria in the story?

WHERE IN THE WORLD?

our world   nature science   pre-reading

Objective: to obtain a mental picture of the globe and to identify the beginning sounds of words.

Materials needed: a large ball, scissors, tape, and the activity sheet (p. 37).

Explain that the earth, where we live, is like a huge ball in the sky. Cut out the countries. (Note: in order to prevent confusion, the countries are labeled with names whose initial sound best matches the phonetic sounds you have probably been teaching your child. We stayed away from words like Europe which starts with an E but sounds like a U.) Call out the name of each country. Let your child listen for the beginning sound.

Find the corresponding letter on one of the countries. Together, tape it on the ball in an approximate location. Show the child where in the world he is living. Note the distances to other places. What countries are near? Which ones are farther away?

FINGER PLAY

drama   physical activity

Objective: to point out that "what you sow, you'll reap."

Teach the following poem with its accompanying hand gestures. Explain the meanings of sowing and reaping. Talk about what the Bible means when it says, "Give and it will be given to you" (Luke 6:38).

> He that sows a little
>   (daintily pluck imaginary seeds from your hand)
> Will have a tiny crop;
>   (measure an inch between thumb and forefinger)
> But if he spreads a lot of seed
>   (throw seeds to the wind)
> He'll reap and never stop.
>   (gather in harvest with both arms)

WEEK TWO

GIVING WHAT YOU HAVE

story   object lesson

Objective: to teach that giving demands sacrifice.

Materials needed: two small bowls, one with flour, the other with oil.

Tell the story from 1 Kings 17 about the woman who had only a little bit of flour and oil left. Show the small bowls. Ask what your child would have done if that's all the food he had left.

Elijah was God's preacher. But one day Elijah was very hungry and thirsty. The land where he lived was dry and hot. Rain had not fallen for many years. How would God take care of Elijah when the trees were withered, the animals were dying, the streams were dry, and the crops were shriveled?

God chose a poor widow woman to help Elijah. This woman did not have a big house or a lot of food, but God could see her heart and knew that she was loving and giving.

As Elijah walked up the dusty road to Zarapheth, he could see the woman stooped over, gathering sticks to make a fire. As he came closer, he called out, "May I have a little drink of water?" The widow hurried to get the pot that held her water. Elijah called out after her, "While you are getting the water, could I also have a piece of bread?"

The woman turned around to face the prophet. She said, "God knows, I don't even have any bread to give you. As a matter of fact, I only have a little flour and oil in the bottom of my jars, and I was collecting this firewood to put in my stove to make a little pancake as a last meal for me and my son. After it is gone, we die."

But Elijah encouraged the woman. He said, "Make the pancake as you planned, but give me some first. I assure you if you will only give to others first, God will refill your flour and oil jar over and over until the rain falls on this land again.

You can imagine what a hard choice it was for the woman. What if Elijah was wrong? What if he was lying? Then she would have foolishly given away all her food. But the woman was used to giving, even when it meant she had none for herself. Without complaint, she prepared the meal and offered it to the preacher. Already, there was enough left for her and her son. After that day, every time she peeked into the jars, she saw enough flour and oil to make one more cake. God gave to her because she gave to others.

FINGER PUPPETS

drama

Objective: to reinforce the lesson that we should give what we can, even if it is very small.

Materials needed: scissors, tape, and the activity sheet (p. 39).

Reenact the Bible story. Follow the instructions on the activity page with an emphasis on the fact that the woman never would have received a miracle from God if she had not been willing to give.

FOOD GROUPS

our world   nature science

Objective: to get a casual grasp of the idea of different food groups.

Materials needed: cardboard box, scissors, marking pen, and the activity sheet (p. 41).

Talk about the four groups of foods: dairy, meat, grains, and fruits and vegetables. If you like, bring representatives from pantry and 'fridge to illustrate each category. Follow the directives on the activity sheet and see if your child can remember what you have taught. Under what category would you place the food that the woman served to Elijah?

PICK UP STICKS

pre-math   game

Objective: to carry out the theme of food and add up countable items.

Materials needed: Uncooked spaghetti noodles.

Remember what the woman was doing when Elijah first saw her. Play a game of "Pick-Up-Sticks" with the spaghetti. Throw the sticks in a disheveled pile on the floor. See how many sticks your child can pick up, one at a time, without moving the other sticks in the jumble. It's your turn when he accidentally bumps any stick other than the one he is trying to pick up. Let your child count to see who has the greatest number of sticks at the end of the game.

THE MUFFIN MAN

concepts   skill   activity

Objective: to contrast *hungry* and *full* by experiencing both.

Materials needed: 3/4 cup milk, 1/2 cup oil, 1 egg, 1 cup raisins, 1 cup flour, 1/3 cup sugar, 1 cup quick-cooking oats, 1 Tb. baking powder, 1 tsp. salt, and a greased muffin tin.

Beat milk, oil, and egg. Stir in raisins. In another bowl, combine flour, oats, sugar, baking powder, and salt. Stir together the wet and dry ingredients until just moistened. Pour into muffin cups. Bake in 400° oven for 18-20 minutes until golden brown. Makes 1 dozen. As you are waiting for the muffins to bake, talk about how *hungry* you are. Think of Elijah and how hungry he must have been. What if these muffins were the only meal you had eaten in hours? How would they taste? After you eat the muffins, do you feel *full*?

WEEK THREE

COLOR BLENDING

story   lesson   crafts

Objective: to learn about primary and secondary colors and to see that giving demands total involvement.

Materials needed: yellow, blue, and red paint (tempera or watercolor), white paper, and a paintbrush.

Tell the following story. When you talk about the color characters, make a swipe on the paper with the color they represent.

When the blue blends with red, brush the two colors together on the page to see what color they will become. Do the same with yellow/blue and red/yellow.

Once upon a time, there were only three colors in the world. Each one thought that she was the best. Blue paraded around, boasting about how her color painted the sky and water. She bragged, "You can see me everywhere you look. I am the most important."

But Yellow was not to be outdone. She pushed in front of Blue and hissed, "Your color is much too cold. Just look at the sunbeams and dancing daisies I have painted. The world is much better because of me."

Then Red danced in front of Yellow and stated proudly, "Animals and people could never do without me. They need blood to live, and I am the color of the rich liquid that flows through their veins. I am also the color of fire, another important thing to mankind."

And so day after day the colors argued until one afternoon they stood looking over a meadow. Something just didn't seem to look right. They all agreed. The grass was pale and faint and although some of the flowers were yellow, the rest looked downright dull. "I'll color the grass," suggested Blue.

"Oh, no," the others protested, "blue sky and blue grass would be too boring."

"How about me?" cried Red. "A field of brilliant red would be very dramatic."

The others shook their heads, "Too startling. It would look like the grass was on fire."

"Then I'm the only one left," declared Yellow triumphantly. "Yellow grass rippling across a meadow would look very cheerful."

But Blue and Red disagreed, "Yellow in moderation is not bad. But a whole field of it is just too much."

Finally Red had a new idea. "You know what we might try? What if two of us blended together? Maybe we could make a new color. Here, Blue," she prompted, "put a little color on this blade of grass. Then Yellow, you dab a little bit of yourself on top, and let's see what happens."

But Blue held back. "I'm just not sure," she said with a slight tilt of her head. "I've always been a separate color all by myself. I don't know if I want to give some of myself away." But finally the other two convinced her, and the experiment began.

First a splat of blue. Then a dab of yellow. The three moved back to look and cried out in delight. What they saw was a beautiful shade of green. "That looks wonderful," Blue declared. "Let's do the whole valley."

After every leaf and stalk was covered in different variations of green, they tried mixing red and blue to get purple. Then they matched yellow and red to get orange. They used a splash of purple on several clumps of flowers and scattered the orange across the meadow on a plant here and there. The effect was beautiful. But they had to agree. It never could have been done if they had not been willing to share of themselves.

SHAPELY COLORS

Objective: to put certain colors in their proper places.

Materials needed: colored construction paper, scissors, glue, and the activity page (p. 43).

Trace the geometric shapes from the activity sheet onto appropriate colored construction paper. Let your child cut them out and glue them where they belong. Go to your own window and talk about the colors and shapes you can view. Thank the Lord for giving you a world full of color.

CEREAL BACKS

Objective: to differentiate between *front* and *back*.

Materials needed: cereal boxes.

Recall when one color in the character story pushed in front of the others to look more important. Use that reference to introduce this exercise about *front* and *back*. Put on a table all the boxes of cereal that you can muster from the cupboard. Throw in whatever other boxes you can find as well... rice, tapioca, baking soda, etc. Have your child arrange the boxes with all the fronts facing forward. Then scramble the boxes and let him turn all the backs toward himself.

WHERE'S THE LETTER?

Objective: to match colors, demonstrate front and back , and identify alphabetical letters.

Materials needed: colored marking pens and a piece of paper.

With different colored markers, write some letters on the front of a sheet of paper. On the back, write the same letters in the same colors. Set the markers and the page before your child. Call out a letter. Have him find it, circle it with the same color marking pen, turn the sheet over, and find and circle it again. Review the character story about colors.

WRAPPING PAPER

Objective: to use colors to make something practical for gift giving.

Materials needed: Styrofoam meat trays, scissors, tempera paint, brush, glue, and large sheets of paper (perhaps the inside of a paper grocery bag).

Cut a design out of one tray and glue it on the back of another tray. Brush or dip the design in paint and print on the oversized paper. Rinse each tray in water before using another color. Imprint the same design in different colors all over the paper. Let it dry. Use as wrapping paper. Talk about the character story and what your child could possibly share or give away to someone else.

WEEK FOUR

UNSELFISH CHOICES

story   object lesson

Objective: to present the idea of giving up what you want instead of bickering.
Materials needed: toy from your child's toy box.

Tell the following story found in Genesis 14. Preface it by asking your child to imagine a friend coming over to visit. Pretend your child reached for a toy (the one you selected for this lesson), at the same time the other child grabbed for it. The other kid screamed and your child shouted, "It's mine!" Ask your child what he would do next. From there, go right into the story.

"Get your dirty old sheep out of our watering trough!" the angry herdsman shouted. He gave the other man a shove. "Get out and stay out!"

Abraham's shepherds discussed the problem that night around the campfire. "We go to a lot of work to draw water up from the well. Lot's men ought to draw their own water. We are not Lot's servants, even if he is the nephew of our boss," they decided firmly.

When Abraham heard the story, he had to agree there was a problem. But he shook his head when the shepherds argued that they ought to be angry at Lot. "We just have too many flocks and people to live so close together," sighed Abraham. "One of us is going to have to move."

But Abraham was a good and generous man who always wanted the best for others. So when he discussed the problem with Lot, he suggested they take a hike to the top of a nearby mountain. From the ridge, Abraham knew they could look around and see on all sides the land God had promised him as a gift. Flinging out his arms to the right and to the left, Abraham said to Lot, "We cannot live together in peace. Pick which direction you would like to go. If you go one way, I'll go the other way."

Lot, however, was a greedy and selfish man. His eyes zoomed in on the greenest and most beautiful valley in the land. It had rivers, trees, lakes, towns, and villages. "I want that part," he said quickly before Abraham could change his mind.

So Abraham turned around to look at what would be left for him. The sandy desert stretched out as far as he could see. "That will be fine," he said. "I'll head the opposite way."

When the shepherds heard about the deal Abraham had made with Lot, they could hardly believe their ears. They were sure Abraham had made a terrible mistake in letting Lot get the best land. But years later, Lot got into terrible trouble in the city where he lived, while Abraham received blessing after blessing after blessing.

SHARING FAMILY LOVE

skill   our world

Objective: to solidify family bonds.
Materials needed: tape recorder.

Talk about how important family was to Abraham. (He would rather sacrifice than cause friction among his relatives.) See if your child can name your family members, immediate and extended. Make a tape for Grandpa, an aunt, or some relative that especially needs a lift. Include songs, verses, interviews, jokes, or whatever. End with your child completing this sentence, "I love you because...." Put the taped greeting and a note in an envelope and mail them off.

FILL IN THE BLANK

pre-reading   story

Objective: to increase vocabulary and learn how to use various words.

Read the following narrative. Let your child insert the missing words. Enjoy the crazy story that develops. Discuss the responsibility we have toward other members of our family.

Once upon a time there was a little _____. She and her family lived in a great big _____. They all had a wonderful time together. They would _____ and _____ all day long.

But one day her brother opened a _____. What should he see inside but a _____. He was scared of (same word) _____s. What should he do? He _____ and ran away.

The family could not find him anywhere. They looked behind the _____ and under the _____. But he was not to be found. Poor little sister. She missed him most of all.

Suddenly, she had an idea. She _____ and _____. Quickly, she ran straight to the _____. There he was, right in the middle. She _____ and told him everything was OK. He could come _____. How nice it was to be together again.

PLACEMENT

word concepts   arts/crafts   paper-work

Objective: to learn the difference between a *mountain* and a *valley*.
Materials needed: paper and crayons.

Draw a curved line on the page to represent a *mountain* overshadowing a *valley* below. Give your child some items to draw, but state where you wish them to be placed. For example, tell him to put a house or a lake in the valley, and draw trees or a train on the mountain slope. Think of the view that Abraham and Lot must have had from the top of the mountain and the end result of the choices that they made that day.

WHO AM I?

drama   our world

Objective: to think about characteristics that apply to each member of the family.
Materials needed: pieces of clothing belonging to each person in your family.

Lay the clothes out on a bed. Let your child sort through and categorize which fit together by deciding to whom they belong. Let him dress up as each family member and do a little charade by imitating that person's most prominent characteristics. Guess what person he is pretending to be.

1. Cut out the finger puppets.
2. With tape, fasten them to your nimblest fingers.
3. Reenact the Bible story of the widow woman and her son, Elijah, and the pots that were never empty.
4. Let your child put on the presentation for you (and whatever audience you can scrounge – neighbors, friends, rest of family, dolls, etc.).

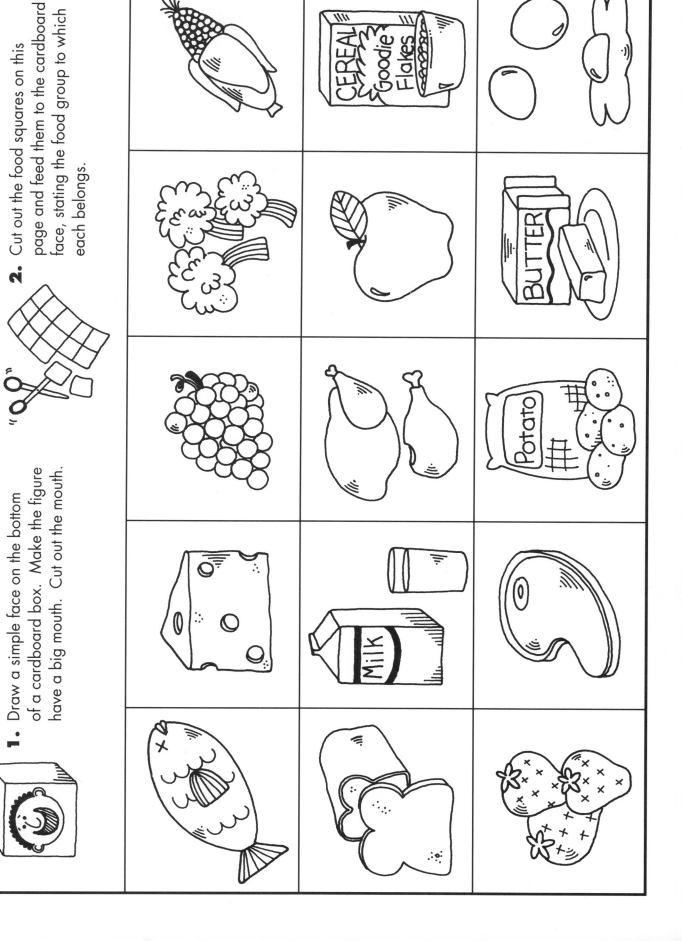

1. Draw a simple face on the bottom of a cardboard box. Make the figure have a big mouth. Cut out the mouth.

2. Cut out the food squares on this page and feed them to the cardboard face, stating the food group to which each belongs.

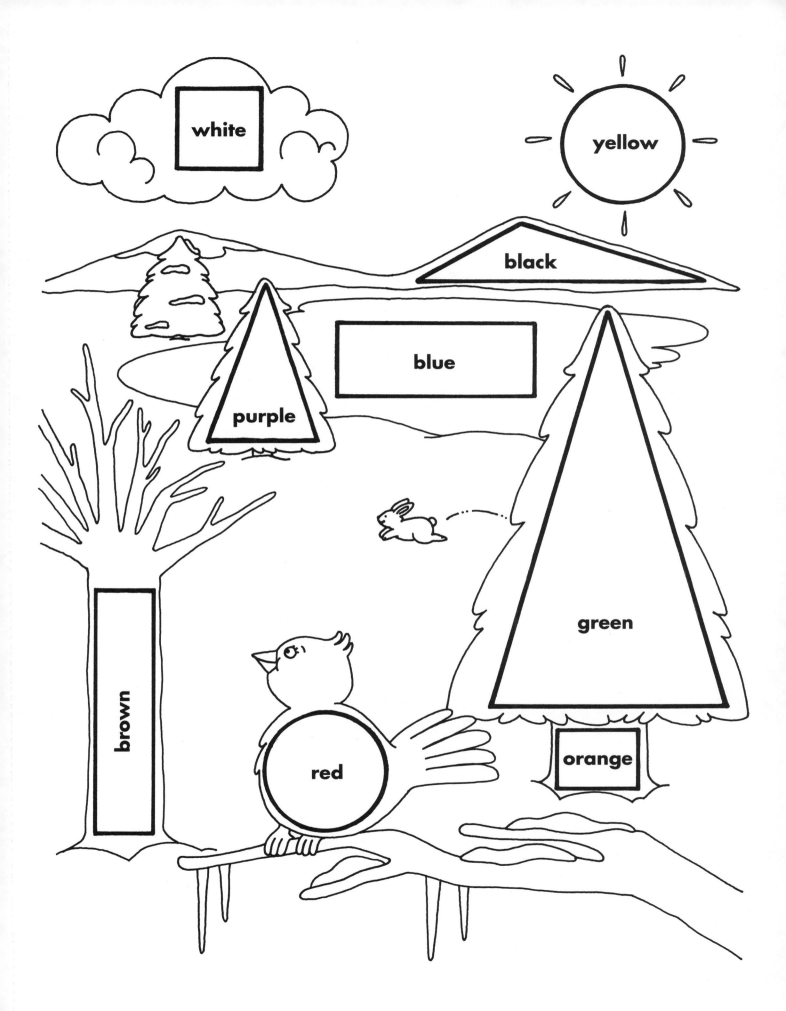

FEBRUARY

WEEK ONE

YOU BROKE IT!

story

world

Objective: to open a forum on anger and forgiveness.

Recall what happened last Mother's Day. Did your family do anything significant together? Did your child give you a card or present that you still have and can look at together with fond memories? Tell the following story, asking your child to put himself in the character's place. What if Ryan had chosen not to forgive?

"It's beautiful!" Mom cried as she looked at the pretty necklace Ryan made for her on Mother's Day. "Would you help me put it on?" Proudly, Ryan tied the string of delicate beads around his mother's neck. It perfectly matched the dress she was wearing to church. He could just imagine the compliments she would receive and how she would smile and murmur, "You know, my son Ryan made it just for me."

His little sister climbed up on mother's lap. "I wike it," Adrian grinned and touched the shiny necklace with a stubby finger. The beads sparkled as she felt their polished surface. But somehow she must have tugged a little too hard, because the thin string broke and the beads slipped off in a rush for the floor. Ryan gave a shout and began scrambling for the runaway beads. "Adrian, you beast!" he screamed. "You broke Mom's present. I worked hard on the necklace. I wanted it to be so nice." Then he sat right in the middle of the pile of beads and burst into tears.

"You know, Ryan," Mom said softly, "as much as I loved that necklace, there is one present you could give me that I would love

just as much." Ryan stopped howling and squinted through his watery eyes. He looked up questioningly at his mom as she explained, "If you would forgive your sister in love, that would just make my day."

Love his sister? Forgive her? After what she did? He looked over at Adrian. She was stretching her chubby little arm as far as it would go under the dresser to reach a bead that she could barely see. It was a choice he would have to make. Yes, if it would please his mother, he could love and forgive. "I'll get that for you," he said to Adrian and easily slid the bead where she could pick it up and place it in a pile with the rest. "Thank you, Ryan," said his mom as she gave him a squeeze. "You have made the Lord and me very proud of you."

FAMILIAR FACES

drama

world

Objective: to make the child see the perspectives of others in his family.
Materials needed: a non-valued photo of each family member, scissors, tape, pencils.

From the photos, cut out the head of each member of the family. Tape each on the end of a pencil and use as a puppet. Let your child put himself in the place of Mom, Dad, Sister, and Brother. Act out the various roles, changing characters every few minutes. Set up the following situations as well as some of your own:

- The washing machine leaks all over the floor.
- The family is deciding where to go on an outing.
- The trash needs to be taken out.
- Mother is not feeling well.
- No one wants to lose at a game.
- Dad gets fired from his job.

MAGNETIC ATTRACTION

Objective: to observe the power of a magnet and compare *thick* and *thin*.

Materials needed: a magnet, a metal object, surfaces with varied thicknesses (paper, cardboard, mirror, book, or tabletop).

Ask your child whether the necklace in the story had a *thick* or *thin* string. Talk about the difference. Observe how the magnet will attract through a thin surface but loses its power when trying to work through something thick. Be amazed and amused.

FORGIVING OTHERS

Objective: to provide an opportunity to count and write numbers and to show how many times a person ought to forgive.

Materials needed: two pieces of paper and a crayon.

Before the lesson, read Matthew 18:21-22, then thoroughly dot one piece of paper with marks. Put the other sheet in front of your child with a crayon. Ask him to make seven marks on the page. Practice writing the number seven. Talk about how Peter came to Christ with a question: "Lord, how often shall my brother sin against me and I forgive him? Up to seven times?" Then show your child the other sheet and ask him to count all the dots. It is an impossible task, but let him go as high as he can. Tell him that Jesus told Peter to forgive as many times as there are dots on the page and even more. Four hundred ninety to be exact. When are good times for your child to practice forgiveness?

HANDLING ANGER

Objective: to decide what behavior is unacceptable and what is appropriate when handling anger.

Materials needed: a pencil and the activity sheet (p. 51).

Look at each picture and decide if the person is doing the right thing to handle anger. Cross out the bad examples. Circle the good. Help your child think of some of the ways he vents frustration. Should these actions be circled or crossed out?

WEEK TWO

CHEERFUL GIVER

Objective: to realize that we cannot worshipfully give without personal sacrifice.

Materials needed: stones, sticks, and a stuffed animal.

Tell the following story from 1 Chronicles 21. To visually explain a sacrifice, use the stones as a foundation, and place the sticks and the animal on top. After you finish the story, talk about how some parents give their children money to put in the offering at church. Are there any chores around the house that your child could do to earn money to give to the Lord each week instead?

David was King of Israel when he decided to build an altar to the Lord and worship Him in a special place. An altar is made out of stones piled together. On top is a stack of wood with an animal. The wood and the animal burn up. But what God is looking for is the giving and loving heart of the person who offers the sacrifice.

The place that David chose to worship God actually belonged to someone else. It was on the top of a big hill. Ornan was the farmer who owned the land.

Imagine Ornan's surprise when he looked up to see the king and a whole company of the king's servants approaching. The king *himself* was on Ornan's land to visit him! He was so overcome that he fell on his face to the ground. "Why did you come here?" he asked timidly.

David explained that he wanted to buy the field from him to offer sacrifices to God. "Oh no," answered Ornan excitedly. "You don't have to buy it from me. I'll just give it to you. And you can have my plows to use as the wood for the altar and the oxen that pull my plows will be fine for the animals to put on top of the wood and…"

But David put out his hand to stop Ornan from continuing. "That is wonderful of you to offer all these things," he said with a smile, "but this is supposed to be *my* sacrifice and there is no way that I can offer to God something that has cost me nothing!"

At the king's insistence, Ornan received fifty silver shekels for the land. David knew something important. If we want to give something to God and to other people, it must cost us something.

PIGGY BANK

Objective: to reinforce the child's resolve to start giving to the Lord.
Materials needed: small empty box, paper, scissors, glue, glitter, paint, and brushes.

Make a bank to hold the money your child will be earning to give to God. Cover the box with paper. Cut a slit in the top. Let the child decorate it with glitter, paints, or whatever he desires.

AMOUNTS

Objective: to differentiate between *more* and *less*.
Materials needed: various containers found around the house that have things in them.

Discuss the piggy bank your child is working to fill. How much money is in it? Place it on a table with a myriad of different containers: juice pitchers, crayon boxes, trash cans, sugar canisters, perfume bottles, and boxes of nails. Let your child state which has *more* in it and which has *less*.

EXIT

Objective: to learn a word that is essential in public places.
Materials needed: four pieces of paper, each with one of the following letters: *E, X, I, T.*

Review the story of David and his sacrifice. Explain that the land he bought eventually became the temple site, a place where Jews from everywhere could come and worship God. Prepare your child for corporate worship in a public building. Introduce the word *EXIT*. Sound out each letter. Mix up the letters and let him practice putting them in the right order. Think of places where this sign can be seen.

WAYS TO WORSHIP

Objective: to see that worship is not limited to a particular time, place, or position.

Discuss the fact that giving is only one aspect of worship. To "worship" means to show God that we love him. We can also worship by singing, talking to others about God, praying, appreciating creation, etc. Play a worship game. Work on finishing this sentence: "I praise God because He...." Sit against the wall of a room. For every new ending, each person turns a somersault. The game is done when you reach the other side of the room.

WEEK THREE

I GO WHERE YOU GO

story   drama   our world   physical activity

Objective: to show that love is always faithful.
Materials needed: colorful sheets or robes.

Dress up like a person from a Middle Eastern nation with flowing robes and headdress. Talk about how climate and custom would affect what a person wears. Go into the story of Ruth and Naomi, residents of Moab. (The story is taken from the Book of Ruth.)

Once there were two women. Ruth and Orpah both lived in Moab. Both had married brothers from Israel. Their husbands died and all they had left to remind them of their wonderful husbands was their mother-in-law, Naomi. Both Ruth and Orpah loved Naomi very much and when Naomi woke up one morning and announced she was moving back to Israel, both girls declared they would go with her.

They were well on their way when Naomi turned to the girls. "You really should go back home," she said. "I don't have anything to offer you. I have no more sons to be your husbands. You'd be better off with our own families." Orpah listened to Naomi's advice and kissed her mother-in-law before turning back to Moab.

But Ruth clung to Naomi. "Don't ask me to leave you," she begged. "I want to go wherever you go. I want to live wherever you live. I want to make your country my country. I want to make your God my God. Wherever you die, I want to die." Naomi could see that Ruth was determined so she didn't try anymore to make her go back home.

When they arrived in Israel, Naomi realized how wonderful it was to have with her a loving young woman like Ruth. Right away Ruth went out to gather food for them to eat. She worked hard for Naomi. Then one day she married a fine man who provided well for both of them.

But the best thing that happened was when Ruth had a baby and Naomi became a grandmother. Oh, how she adored her little grandchild. It made her happy to be alive. Ruth and her faithful, never-ending love gave all of this to Naomi.

NATIONALITIES

our world   arts/crafts   paper-work

Objective: to see how different cultural backgrounds provide a rich heritage.
Materials needed: paper and crayons.

Talk about your own family's history as you consider the difficult time Ruth would have had adjusting to the customs of another country. From your own nationality, share some unique distinctives belonging to the country of your ancestors. Together, create a family "coat of arms." Draw an emblem that includes a blend of your ethnic background and the interesting things the members of your family are involved in now. For example, our family has both a Scottish and an Italian background. We might include in our "coat of arms" a pair of kilts and a plate of spaghetti. Because our family loves to read books, we might choose to draw all our symbolic pictures on the sketch of an open book.

TAKING A TRIP

drama   physical activity

Objective: to consider everything that's involved in taking a trip.
Materials needed: a suitcase.

Plan an imaginary trip. Pack everything that you will need. Assist your child in thinking of the items by himself. (i.e., What will you need to brush your teeth?) Pretend you are actually traveling, using whatever type of transportation you desire. When you arrive, check to see that you remembered everything you need. Think about Ruth and the long trek to her new homeland.

BALLOON MESSAGES

pre-reading   nature science   our world   physical activity

Objective: to review the many ways to communicate over distance and provide some letter writing practice.
Materials needed: balloon, straw, tape, paper, pencil, and string.

List the ways two people can keep in touch even from far away — letters, telephone, flowers, visits, packages, etc. Tie a string between two chairs with a one-inch piece of drinking straw on the line. Write a simple message on a square of paper, tape it to a blown up but not tied balloon. Using a large piece of tape around the center of the balloon, attach it to the straw, let go of the end, and watch it fly from one chair to the other. Help your child decipher your message and write one to you. His greeting does not have to be made up of real words, but encourage him to be forming real letters. Let him explain to you what he wrote after he shoots a balloon message back to you. Is balloon mail a possible method of communicating over a distance?

CHAROSES

skill   our world   physical activity

Objective: to eat a dish that Ruth possibly would have discovered in her new country.
Materials needed: chopped apples, almonds, lemon rind, cinnamon, and a little grape juice.

Talk about the adjustment of moving to a brand-new land...different customs, weather, clothing, religion, and foods. Learn how to make Charoses, a dish that the Israelis eat during the Passover. Take the ingredients and stir them together to represent the brick mixture that the Children of Israel had to make as slaves in Egypt before Moses led them over the Red Sea. Once a year during the Seder feast, this dish is prepared and enjoyed by Jewish people around the world.

WEEK FOUR

SHUNAMMITE WOMAN

story   skill   physical activity

Objective: to see that the best gifts can be something you make yourself.
Materials needed: hammer, nails, and wood.

Let your child hammer a few nails into the wood. Ask what kinds of things you can make out of wood. Tell your child the story, from 2 Kings 4, about a wife and her husband who made a gift out of these very items.

"Won't you please come in and join us for supper?" the woman asked with a smile. Elisha was glad to come into the coolness of her home. Sitting in a comfortable chair, he visited with her husband until dinner was ready. Simple but delicious, it gave him the strength he needed to continue his journey.

After that night, every time Elisha came to town, the woman was sure to invite him in for a meal. She could tell he appreciated the chance to rest and enjoyed the nourishing food. Was there anything else she could do to help this man of God?

One day she had an idea. Excitedly, she talked it over with her husband. What if they should add a room onto their house — a simple set of steps up the side and a square addition on the roof — plus a little bit of furniture and a lamp? Wouldn't Elisha just love it? He could have a place of his own whenever he was in town!

Her husband agreed and they began working right away. It was fun to be able to hammer, cut, paint, and fix up a little place that would be so useful to God's servant. The woman from Shunem had learned the joy of working to make something for someone else.

HOUSE OF CARDS

skill   physical activity

Objective: to provide a chance to review the Bible story while working on hand-eye coordination.
Materials needed: pack of playing cards.

Work together to make a card house by leaning the cards against each other. Show your child how to achieve the precarious balance to form walls and rooms. While you are working, talk about the woman who added a room onto her house for the man of God.

THIS SIDE UP

word concepts   paper-work

Objective: to compare the difference between *above* and *below*.
Materials needed: pencil and the activity sheet (p. 53).

From the story of the woman who built a room above her house for the prophet of God, lead into a comparison of *above* and *below*. Do the activity sheet by matching the view from above with the view from below. State which is which. What is the item you are looking at?

HOSPITALITY

skill   physical activity

Objective: to teach your child what hospitality really means.

Let your child invite a couple of adults over for a visit. Let him be involved in every aspect of the call from deciding who should come, extending the invitation (see next entry), cleaning the house for their arrival, making a snack, asking them to come in, taking their coats, carrying the conversation, etc. Think about how skilled the Shunammite woman must have been at hospitality because she was ready on the spur of the moment to entertain the prophet whenever he was in town.

FORMAL INVITATION

pre-reading   arts/crafts

Objective: to give another opportunity for the formation of letters.
Materials needed: paper and pens.

Let your child draw out an invitation to be used with the guests in the visit previously mentioned. Let him plan the phrasing. Be sure he includes all pertinent points of information. Write his dictated words lightly on the invitation, and instruct your child to write the letters firmly over yours. Decorate as desired.

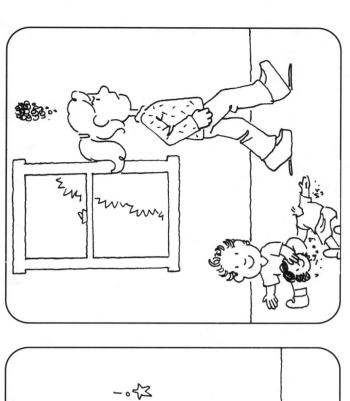

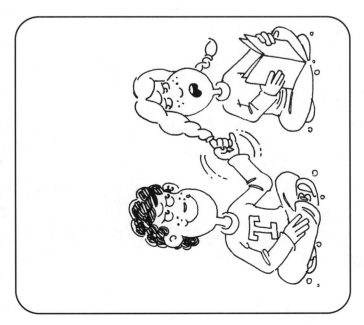

THEME: patience and discernment

INTRODUCTION

I sometimes wonder what it would have been like to be alive during another time period in another country. As a parent, would my feelings for my children or my goals for their lives be any different? What if I were fleeing with my family from German occupation in war-ravaged Europe? What if I lived in a bamboo hut in a tiny village newly evangelized by early missionary endeavors? What if I were the lord of a walled castle staunchly guarding a windswept moor? Going way back, what if I traveled nomadically, pitching my tent in the hot and dusty land of Palestine? Would I face my role as a parent or visualize success in child rearing any differently than I do now?

Clothes, customs, opinions, and panoramas change, but God-serving parents of all ages have sought to develop loving relationships with their children and to build the character of God into their lives. Some were successful. Some were not. But regardless of ability, resource, or surroundings, they were held equally responsible by God for the way their offspring turned out.

Check out the obvious correspondence between the lifestyles of the various kings of Israel and the lifestyles of their parents. Over and over we find testimonials like the following in 1 Kings 15:1-2, "Abijah became king of Judah, and he reigned in Jerusalem three years. His mother's name was Macaah, daughter of Abishalom. He committed all the sins his father had done before him." God's evaluation seems to be, like parent, like child. In New Testament times, a man could not even serve as an elder unless his children were in line and adhering to Christian principles. Scripture unmistakably exhorts parents to bring up their children "in the fear and admonition of the Lord."

We are clearly answerable to God for the way we raise our youngsters, but how can we accomplish this seemingly impossible undertaking? When we take a squirrelly child, bent toward evil and self-will, and throw in a wild-eyed parent, unwitting and idealistic, is it any wonder that we briskly conclude the whole task of child-rearing is a sheer impossibility?

God encourages us to observe our calling from a less sophisticated point of view. Consider the simplicity of the method He suggests to Abraham in Deuteronomy 6:7. God says that no matter what we're doing during the day, (reading a book, going on a walk, working on a project, or eating a meal) and no matter what time it is, (bright and early in the morning or when we finally toddle into bed at night) we should use every experience as a teaching tool to incorporate into our children's lives the things they need to know. Capitalize on every circumstance and opportunity that comes your way. Make practical application. Use whatever you have on hand. Illustrate Biblical truth in parable form. Become the master of the moment.

Every parent is capable of this. We lack only one thing—experience. We hold in our arms an inconsolable baby or chase our disobedient three-year-old around the house or glance into the dirty, sock-infested room of an older child and desperately moan, "What have I brought into this world?" But be assured that experience always tags on the heels of time and practice. We must just jump in.

Supplemental aid is furnished for us in the form of examples. The elderly grandparents of our church flocks provide perfect mentors. God designed that the wisdom they have accumulated as seasoned veterans would be passed on to us in the form of encouragement and counsel (Titus 2:4). We could learn so much if we would just take time to listen.

Additional models are found in the pages of Scripture—positive and negative. Pore over the following passages. Surely the mission we undertook when we decided to be parents is consequential enough to deserve serious study. Scripture contains a vineyard full of knowledge, ripe and tasty, ready to be gleaned.

(1) 2 Timothy 1:5; 3:15. Eunice was probably a single mother, but she employed the assistance of other family members in raising Timothy and succeeded in passing on to him a faith that was "alive."

(2) Luke 1:5-25, 39-45; Matthew 3; 11:2-3. Zacharias and Elizabeth were the parents of John the Baptist. They were strict disciplinarians who instilled in the son of their old age a sense of purpose and a singular focus. (Did Zacharias also pass on a predisposition to doubt when tested?)

(3) Judges 13–16. Mr. and Mrs. Manoah raised their son with the same set of rules as John, but Samson grew up with a complete lack of discipline, a violent temper, and a self-indulgent lifestyle. How can two children have the same outer constraints but develop a totally different character?

(4) Exodus 2:1-15; Hebrews 11:23-28. Moses' parents did not allow the decadence of their generation to change their personal convictions. Let the other Hebrew parents hand their babies over to be murdered; they believed that life inferred destiny. They used the preschool years of Moses' life to instill in him faith and a sense of family and heritage that would last for a lifetime.

(5) Matthew 20:20-28. The mother of James and John was outgoing and aggressive when it came to the success of her two sons. Called the "Sons of Thunder" (Do you think they found themselves in and out of trouble when growing up?), they always depended on Mom to get for them what they wanted.

(6) Acts 16:14-15. Lydia was so honored and revered in her household that when she decided to follow God, everyone else in her family made the same choice too. Now that's the way to be influential!

(7) Genesis 5:32; 7:13; 9:18-27. Noah learned a lesson the hard way when God put a special curse on one of his sons. He found that whatever a parent allows in moderation, the children will try in excess. Noah's lack of restraint in drinking demonstrated itself in Ham as a lack of restraint in the area of morality.

(8) Exodus 3:1, 18-20; 18. Jethro demonstrated how advice and instruction continues to be important even after our children are grown and gone. He shared some wisdom that would benefit not only his own daughter Zipporah, but also his son-in-law Moses and the whole system of government in all of Israel. The advice we give may have far-reaching implications. Even idle words are important.

(9) 1 Samuel 2:12-17; 3:11-14; 4:11, 18. Eli was the unreliable and inconsistent parent of Hophni and Phineas. Perhaps Eli's severe weight problem caused the boys to question the authority of their father. At any rate, they grew up to be totally disrespectful and immoral. God rebuked Eli's inability to discipline and judged his descendants forever.

(10) Genesis 25:21-28; 26:34-35; 27:1-17. Isaac and Rebekah were the parents of twin boys. Their first mistake was favoritism, each parent coddling and encouraging the child he or she liked the best. Rebekah made a second error when she encouraged Jacob to deceive his father in order to get what he wanted. The consequence followed immediately. Mother and child were separated, never to see each other again.

What a heritage we have in such real-life examples. Our challenge is to learn from these and the other down-to-earth models that God has positioned in our paths at this time. What a perfect system God ordained when He encouraged us to involve our children in our day-to-day experiences and duties. This doesn't mean simply seeking ways to amuse them or get them out of our hair, as if we must figure out what to do with them, but rather using our own lives as the means to teach character and virtue. That is our highest calling. *Lord, prepare us for the exertion that this demands, then allow us to experience the exhilaration of success.*

MARCH
WEEK ONE

WAITING FOR RAIN

 story object lesson arts/crafts

Objective: to illustrate the patience required in waiting for answers to prayer.

Materials needed: construction paper, crayons, cotton balls, and glue.

Tell the story of Elijah on Mr. Carmel as found in 1 Kings 18. After the story, trace your child's hand onto the construction paper. Within the outline, glue pieces of cotton to look like a cloud the size of a hand. Hold the finished paper up and ask your child if he would have been sure of God's answer when the cloud was still so small. Patience believes that God is at work even when the evidence is slim.

As long as the Israelites continued to forget God, there was no rain, not one drop, in all the land. Finally, on the top of Mt. Carmel, the Israelites turned from their sins and decided to serve the Lord once more. After this, most of the people returned to their homes, but Elijah, God's man, fell on his knees and began to pray for the rain to come.

Have you ever prayed for something and it seemed as if it took God a long time to answer? Well, that's the way it was for Elijah. He asked his servant to look out over the sea and tell him if he saw any clouds. The servant returned and said the sky was crystal clear. But Elijah did not give up. He kept praying for rain. He talked to God for a little bit and then sent his servant down again to look for any sign of a storm. Each time the man returned and said that he saw nothing. Finally, on the seventh try, the servant called to Elijah that he saw a tiny cloud, just the size of a man's hand, way out to sea.

That was all Elijah needed to hear. He knew God had answered his prayer. Hollering back to the servant to come quickly, Elijah gathered up the folds of the clothes he was wearing and ran as fast as he could to safety. A storm was coming. The heavens grew black, the winds howled, and the rain fell in torrents.

Elijah had not given up. He had been patient in prayer and the Lord had answered.

WEATHER STATION

 nature science our world physical activity

Objective: to become more aware of changes in weather and how weather affects us.

Materials needed: cup, ruler, stick, sock, washcloth, and an outdoor thermometer.

Be creative in setting up a miniature station to gauge the weather. Use a cup to catch and mark rainfall, a ruler to measure depth of snow, a sock on a stick to indicate the direction of the wind, a washcloth to catch dew, and a thermometer to read the temperature. Observe and marvel over the discoveries you make.

RAINDROP PATTERNS

 word concepts arts/crafts our world

Objective: to work with *wet* and *dry* materials and contrast the difference.

Materials needed: paper towels, water, an oversized, old shirt or a smock, and food coloring.

Cover your child to protect his clothes. Place a paper towel on the table. Splat some drops of food coloring onto the paper towel one drop at a time and watch the paper absorb the liquid. Sprinkle some water onto the same towel one drop at a time. What happens to the colors? Talk about Elijah and how he must have felt when the first *wet* sprinkles touched his skin after such a long *dry* period in the land.

BRAVING THE ELEMENTS

pre-reading   our world   paper-work

Objective: to introduce the different kinds of weather and the first letter of each.

Materials needed: pencil and the activity sheet (p. 67).

Look at the child in each picture. Decide what type of weather pattern is occurring in each one. Listen for the beginning sound of each word. Have your child write the letter in the blank. Find the picture that best matches the weather you are experiencing today. Thank God for it.

WATER MUSIC

music   physical activity

Objective: to use a natural phenomenon to make harmonious sounds.

Materials needed: water and an assortment of containers (differing in size and material).

Create a symphony of sorts by dripping water into the containers. Listen to the different plops and smacks that you can make. Does the height from which you release the drops or how much water is present in the bottom of the container change the tune? How did these same kinds of sounds signify many years ago to Elijah that his prayer was answered? Is there anything for which you are waiting on God at this present time?

BREAKING A BONE

story   drama   object lesson   nature science   our world

Objective: to present healing as a process during which a person must practice patience.

Materials needed: swatches of cloth.

Read the following story about the little girl who breaks an arm. Play doctor together. Pretend your child fractures a limb. Wrap it up and instruct the child to wait a little while before removing the bandages.

The pain was worse than anything Jennie had ever felt before. She cradled her arm and moaned. She wanted to scream, but the nurse was asking her to lie still on the table until the doctor came into the room.

After a special camera took a picture of her arm, the doctor knew for sure it was a break. He pointed it out to her parents with a pencil on a lighted board. Then the doctor gave Jennie a shot that felt like a small prick and made the pain go away almost at once. Finally, he was able to set the arm and make it stiff in a plaster cast.

"How long do I have to wear this?" Jennie asked when the cast hardened as solid as a rock. She was thinking how difficult it would be to play and take a bath with something like that on her arm.

The doctor grinned. "It will be four to six weeks, I'm afraid. But just be patient and you'll see the time will go a lot faster than you think." Jennie rolled her eyes. Four to six weeks seemed like a lifetime. Wasn't there an easier way?

When she got home, Jennie rested just like the doctor told her. Her mother handed her some books on bones to look through. As Jennie pored over the pictures, she was amazed to see that in order for the crack in her bone to heal, one broken piece must actually grow together again with the other. Her body had a lot of work to do! All of a sudden the six weeks didn't seem as long as it had before. She would eat well, get lots of rest at night, play hard, and exercise in the way the doctor advised. In the meantime, God would be working on the inside, healing and knitting those broken bones back together in a way that would make her arm even stronger than before. She would be patient and wait.

HEAVYWEIGHT

Objective: to make comparisons between *heavy* and *light*.

Materials needed: a scale and various heavy and light items.

Key off the broken arm story to talk about the strength of our bodies when healthy. Compare the differing weights of the objects you have chosen. Note that the higher the number on the scale, the more difficult an item is to lift. Use the words *heavy* and *light* to describe the difference.

HEALTH AND HEALING

Objective: to open a forum for discussion on the many kinds of treatments to facilitate healing.

Review the familiar nursery rhyme until you can quote it together.

**Jack and Jill went up a hill
to fetch a pail of water.
Jack fell down and broke his crown
and Jill came tumbling after.
Jack got up and home did trot
as fast as he could caper.
He went to bed and wrapped his head
in vinegar and brown paper.**

What are some other things a doctor or nurse might suggest to help a sick person get well?

A MOUTHFUL

Objective: to give an opportunity to count something related to the theme of health.

Let your child count all the teeth in his mouth. Use a mirror if necessary. Have him count the teeth in your mouth. How many more teeth do you have? Explain the process of losing baby teeth to get full-sized replacements. How can teeth be properly cleaned to maintain a healthy mouth?

CLEANLINESS NEXT TO GODLINESS

Objective: to promote the thought that sanitation is a good step toward vitality and health.

Materials needed: dish soap and two drinking straws.

Pull up a stool so your child can reach into the kitchen sink. Do dishes together with a tub of warm water and lots of bubbles. Let your child handle all the unbreakable dishes while you finish off the rest. Take the straws and blow into the detergent water to watch the bubbles multiply. While play/working, talk about the importance of eating off clean plates and keeping food and all it touches washed and spotless.

WEEK THREE

WAITING TO SEE

story   game   physical activity

Objective: to present another case where patience is required—waiting to rejoin someone you love.

Before you tell the story of Paul and his lonely letters from jail (read Acts 16 and Philippians 1), play a modified version of "Red Rover." Let your child stand on one side of the room against the wall. You should stand against the opposite wall. Call out, "Red rover, red rover, send (*insert child's name*) right over." The child must run across the room and try to touch the wall on your side. You should hold out your arms and try to block him from reaching the wall. (If more than two people are playing, let the extras join the one that is defending the wall and call together for the child to come over). Reverse the play and let the child call you by placing your name in the summons. Use this game to introduce the story of Paul's Macedonian call.

One night, Paul had a very strange dream. There was a man in the far-off country of Macedonia calling to him and saying, "Come over to us in our country. Help us!"

When he awoke the next morning, Paul felt so strongly about the dream that he and his friend Silas packed up their belongings right away and caught a ship that was sailing to Macedonia. They landed in a city called Philippi. Along the banks of a river, they met many people who were just waiting to hear about Jesus.

Paul and Silas worked, prayed, and taught for some time in that city. They made many close friends and learned to love the people dearly.

But one day some evil men beat Paul and Silas and threw them in prison for talking about Jesus. They were finally let go but with many warnings from the authorities that they should speak no more about Christ. Paul and Silas felt that it was time to leave. They hugged and kissed their friends before saying good-bye.

Years later, Paul wrote his friends in Philippi a long letter. He was writing from a country far away—once more in jail for talking about Jesus. He told his friends how much he wanted to see them. He remembered the good times they had had together long ago. He missed them very much. If God allowed him, he would come again for a visit, but in the meantime, he explained that he must wait patiently until he was free.

Being separated from friends and waiting longingly to be together again is difficult. Paul knew that, but he also knew that while they waited, both he and his friends would be learning and growing stronger in the Lord.

COMMUNICATION LINE

one world   object lesson

Objective: to look at the many methods of transferring information.

Materials needed: as many of the following items as you can gather: videotape, newspaper, letter, transistor radio, photo, audio cassette, drawing, telephone, musical instrument, and a book.

Define communication as "giving a message to somebody else." Hold up each of the items you have collected, one at a time. How does it pass on a message? Which is the method that Paul used in the Bible story? If you wanted to reach the most number of people, which type of communication would you use?

BABY-SITTING

concepts **world** **game** **activity**

Objective: to quell any fear that a parent will *go* somewhere, never to *return.*

Set your child in front of a solid chair. Slip behind the chair and pop out from either of the two sides or the top. Let your child guess where you will next appear by pointing at the side from which he expects to see your head. Repeat this activity several times. After the game, discuss the fact that Mom and Dad will sometimes *go* away for short periods of time (maybe asking a "caregiver" to watch the youngster), but they will always *return* in a little while. Remind your child about Paul, the man who wrote the lonely letter from jail to his friends in Philippi. God eventually allowed him to be able to return and visit with the people he loved and longed to see.

A TISKET, A TASKET

reading **game** **activity**

Objective: to practice writing skills and learn a new letter (or perfect a familiar one).
Materials needed: paper, string, pencil, and an envelope.

Work on making a nice letter to be used in the game. Put it in an envelope. (Think about the letter that Paul wrote to his friends in Philippi as you labor over yours.) Form a good-sized circle out of the string on the floor. The parent should sit in the middle and sing or recite the following ditty as the child circles (envelope in hand) around the outside of the string:

A tisket, a tasket, a green and yellow basket.
I wrote a letter to my love and on the way I dropped it.
I dropped it, I dropped it, and on the way I dropped it.
A little boy picked it up and put it in his pocket.

When you come to the part of the poem where the letter is dropped, instruct your child to drop his letter and run. You must follow and touch him. If he runs completely around the circle back to where the letter was dropped without being tagged, you must return to the middle. If you tag your child, he takes your place in the middle. (If more than two people play, everyone should sit around the edge of the circle. The child drops the letter behind whomever he chooses and that person must be the one to chase him.)

FOREIGN MISSIONS

world **lesson**

Objective: to picture the mystique and intrigue of other countries in relation to Paul's missionary call.
Materials needed: foreign articles.

Look around your home for things made in other countries. (Read some labels; you may be surprised at the number of articles you find.) Show your child wonderful treasures from far away — a cup from China, a sweater from Scotland, a rug from Turkey, or a tin from Switzerland. Talk about how people from other countries need Jesus just like we do. Will they hear about the Lord if no one goes to tell them?

WEEK FOUR

I'M TIRED OF WAITING

story **lesson** **activity**

Objective: to present the getting-ready process as a time to patiently wait.

Take your child into the bathroom, and review all the things he would do to get ready to go out somewhere: brush teeth, wash face, comb hair, etc. Help him to remember times when he may have been impatient while waiting for someone else to dress and become presentable. With this introduction, read the following story.

"Will you hurry up?" the teeth growled at the hair. "We've been brushed and clean for fifteen minutes now, and you still look as much like a bird's nest as when we first got up this morning."

"Hold yer horses," mumbled the hair as it flopped from one side to the other. "A person can only do one thing at a time, and now he's washing the face."

"But we don't have anything to do," the teeth continued to complain. "It's boring to have to wait for such a long time. We want to go somewhere and do something. If only we could leave without you."

By now, the teeth were so impatient they were chattering a mile a minute and when they got the chance, they would nibble on a fingernail or two. At last the boy was dressed and ready to work on the hair. He carefully pulled the comb through all the knots and snarls. "It's about time!" the teeth snapped disagreeably. "We've been waiting forever."

The next day, the boy decided to comb his hair first. The shining hair grinned down at the teeth who were just starting to work on breakfast. "Now who's waiting for whom?"

DRESSING UP

concepts   skill   activity   world

Objective: to differentiate between *casual* and *dressy* attire.
Materials needed: clothing and accessories.

Set out a diversity of attire: thongs, necklace, shorts, baseball cap, high heels, T-shirt, tie, etc. Let your child pick out and put on everything that would be appropriate to wear on a *dressy* or formal occasion. Put all the clothes back, then direct your child to choose and wear what would be acceptable for a more *casual* setting.

PAPER DOLLS

world   concepts   drama

Objective: to show that there are different times for different clothes.
Materials needed: scissors, crayons, glue, light cardboard, and the activity sheet (p. 69).

The parent should mount the main figure and the base on light cardboard and cut out all the outfits. Your child can color as desired. Do some make-believe play together, setting up situations and dressing the doll appropriately. Would the doll act any differently in the park, wearing play clothes than he would all dressed up at a banquet?

TELLING TIME

math   world   work

Objective to present the basics of time-reading and the approximate times of daily events.
Materials needed: paper plate, brad, scissors, glue, and the activity sheet (p. 71).

Let your child cut out the clock and mount it on a paper plate. Fasten the hands with the brad. Teach your child how to read the short hand only, if telling time is a new concept. Advance to the rudiments of the long hand if your child has already had some experience with telling time. Move the discussion into daily events and glue the pictured squares nearest the times when they usually occur. Talk about the importance of promptness and reliability.

WAITING ON ICE

game

Objective: to give a list of possible things to do while waiting on other people.

Materials needed: ice cube tray, paper, and pencil.

Write the following situations on slips of paper. Fold each piece and put it in a separate compartment of the ice cube tray. Let your child pick any slip and hand it to you. Read out loud what is written on the paper, then talk together about what a kid could do in that situation to make the time go faster. What can you do while waiting for...

(1) food to be served in a restaurant
(2) Dad to get off the phone
(3) an item to be rung up in a check-out line
(4) Mom to finish a chore so she can read a story
(5) morning to come and the family to get up
(6) dinner to be ready
(7) parents to finish talking at church
(8) a trip in the car to be over
(9) a holiday to arrive
(10) the rain to stop so you can go outside
(11) someone special to come over
(12) a long prayer to be finished

Here is one suggestion for each situation. While you wait you can...

(1) borrow paper and pencil and draw a picture
(2) softly sing a favorite song
(3) look for all the things of one color
(4) read a story you know to a stuffed animal
(5) imagine you are a pirate or a princess
(6) set the table
(7) ask an older person to tell you about himself
(8) read license plate letters
(9) count each day on a calendar
(10) do a puzzle
(11) make a picture to give them when they arrive
(12) think of favorite people and ask God to help them

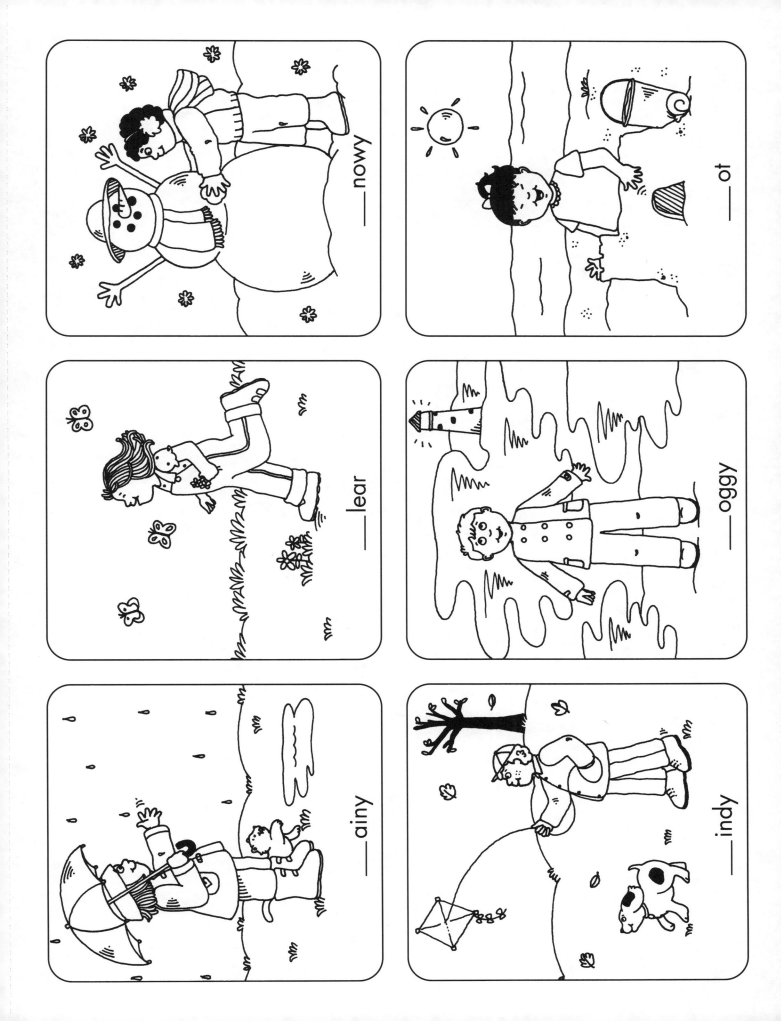

____nowy

____ot

____lear

____oggy

____ainy

____indy

Mount the boy and the base on light cardboard. Cut out the figure and clothes.

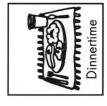
Getting up

Breakfast

Lunchtime

Dinnertime

Doing chores

Time to read

Prayer time

Bath time

Playtime

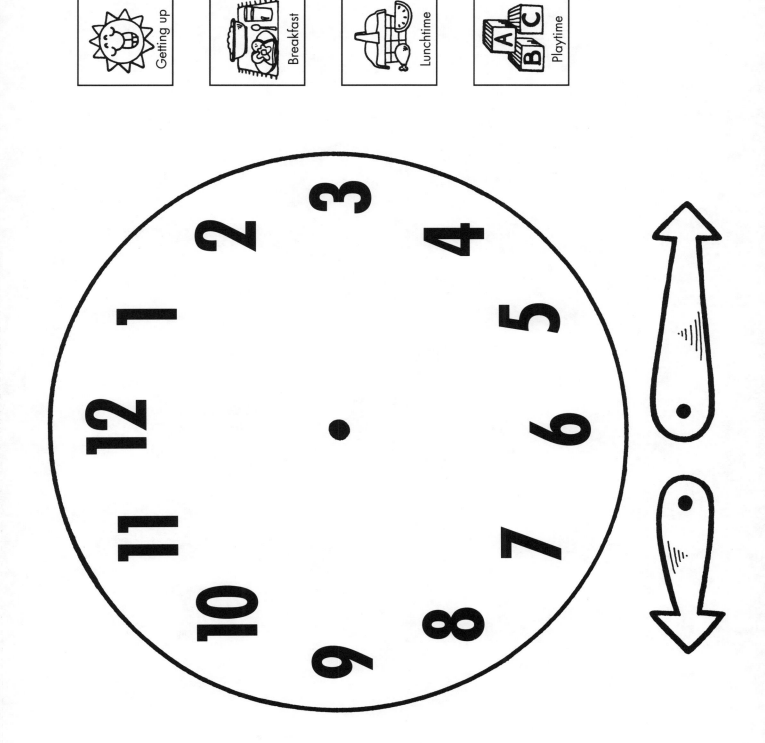

APRIL
WEEK ONE

A GOOD LISTENER

story   our world

Objective: to show that discernment means seeing what is most important and focusing on that.

Begin your time together by being quiet and listening for a few seconds. What different sounds can you hear? Tell the story of Mary and Martha, found in Luke 10. After you have finished, make a list of all the times a person should stop and listen so as to not miss out on something special. For example: a bird singing, a story being read, an orchestra in concert, a tree rustling, etc.

"Mary, you haven't swept the floor," scolded Martha irritably. "You shouldn't sit around talking when you have so much work to do." Martha twitched out of the room with an armful of dirty dishes.

Mary's eyes dropped. Jesus didn't come every day to visit, and He had been telling her some wonderful things about God. Should she really be doing something else instead?

The next time Martha bustled into the room, she started right in. "Jesus," Martha began again, "tell Mary to help me with all the things we need to get done."

"Martha, Martha," Jesus answered calmly and waved at a chair nearby as if to ask her to join them, "you are upset and worried about so many things. But actually, there is only one thing that is important right now. Learning about God is so much better than fluttering around doing this and that. Mary has been discerning. She has seen that what you cook will be quickly eaten and what you clean will soon be dirty. But the God you can get to know will be a friend that will last forever."

TAFFY PULL

skill   physical activity

Objective: to encourage family unity and togetherness.

Materials needed: 1 cup sugar, 1 tbs. cornstarch, 3/4 cup light corn syrup, 2/3 cup water, 2 tbs. butter, 1 tsp. salt, 2 tsp. vanilla, buttered shallow pan, scissors, and a saucepan.

Recall the story about the disagreement between the two sisters Mary and Martha. Do the children in your family ever squabble, or does your child ever argue with a friend? How can cooperation be encouraged? Do a project together that requires unity and working together.

Combine the sugar and cornstarch in a saucepan. Stir in corn syrup, water, butter, and salt. Heat to boiling over medium heat, stirring constantly. Cook, stirring occasionally for about 30 minutes until you can drop a little piece of the taffy into cold water and it forms a ball. Stir in vanilla and pour into the shallow pan. Let it cool about 15 minutes until cool enough to handle. Butter your hands, pull off a section of the candy and pull and twist until it changes color and becomes stiff. Work with another person, stretching and turning the substance between you. Pull into strips 1/2" wide, cut with scissors into 1 1/2" pieces. Wrap the individual pieces in waxed paper.

SOFT ANSWERS

word concepts   physical activity

Objective: to define the difference between *calm* and *upset* and to learn a principle that will prevent anger.

Learn Proverbs 15:1 with accompanying motions. "A gentle answer (quietly stated, putting finger to lips) turns away (push aside with hands) wrath (frown). But a harsh word (shouted, with hands cupped to mouth) stirs up (stir like a spoon in a mixing bowl) anger (clench fists)." Think of the two different responses Mary could have given when Martha criticized and scolded her in front of Jesus: *calm* and *upset*. Which one would have been right?

A DOZEN EGGS

prep
math

arts/
crafts

our
world

Objective: to give opportunity to count an unusual item.
Materials needed: paint, brushes, and twelve hard-boiled eggs.

Color the eggs in bright colors with various designs. Let them dry. Put back into the carton. While you're working, talk about how holidays are wonderful times to encourage traditions and bring families closer together. Give directions and let your child count and display the answers. Ask for things like, "Count and show me all the eggs with a red dot." Or, "Now tell me how many eggs have blue stripes." Make sure when you are painting the eggs that you pattern them with enough variety yet also enough continuity that you are supplied with many possible suggestions.

SEEING THROUGH THINGS

our
world

paper-
work

Objective: to see that discernment means taking a second look to see what's really there.
Materials needed: scissors and the activity sheet (p. 79).

Cut along the dotted line. Place the left-hand side on top of the right. Have your child state what he sees. Now hold the two pages up to a window. Now what does he see? Use this as a basis to review what discernment means. When would it be good to have discernment?

THE BIGGER PICTURE

story

Objective: to see that God has a plan behind even the bad things in life.

Tell the story about Joseph found in Genesis 37–45. What good could come out of the following situations:
(1) falling down and scraping a knee
(2) grandparents living far away
(3) losing some money
(4) dropping an ice cream cone
(5) not winning in a contest

Joseph was a ruler in a great land. He looked down at his brothers as they bowed in front of his throne. They had come to his country to fill their empty bags of grain. There was no food left in the place where they lived. But the brothers did not know who Joseph was because many years had passed since they had last seen him.

The memories flooded Joseph's head. The last time they had been together, the brothers had hatefully thrown him into a deep pit. They had spoken roughly to him. They had laughed nastily when he asked for something to eat or drink. When some evil strangers came by on the road, the brothers sold him as a slave. What a terrible thing to do to your own brother!

It would have been so easy for Joseph to hate them. Now that he was on the throne, he had the power to throw them in jail and even kill them if he liked. But Joseph was not that kind of man. Instead of being angry, he looked at the brothers lovingly. Joseph had the discernment to see that when the brothers tried to do him harm, God worked it out for the best. God had made him a ruler in a great land. So he had no bitterness in his heart. He could forgive.

"Look at me!" he cried. "I am your own brother Joseph. And I am very happy to see you." He filled their empty sacks until they were full of grain.

LEMONADE

word concepts   skill   physical activity

Objective: to provide a basis of referral for the concepts *empty* and *full*.
Materials needed: four lemons, 1/2 cup sugar, 3 cups water, sieve, and two pitchers.

Look into the pitcher. Is it *empty* or *full?* Squeeze 1 cup lemon juice into the pitcher. Is it empty or full? Pour the juice through a sieve into another pitcher. Is it empty or full? Mix the water and sugar in the original container. Is it empty or full? Add to the lemon juice. Is it empty or full?

COMMUNITY HELPERS

our world   drama   physical activity

Objective: to see that we need the people God has placed in our lives and to be grateful for them.

What would the starving brothers have done without Joseph? What would any of the other citizens have done without his leadership and the help of his staff? Talk about how important community helpers are to us. Could we get along without storekeepers, doctors, mail carriers, restaurant servers, etc.? Play a little game of charades by imitating different community helpers. Let the other person guess the role being portrayed.

COLOR BY NUMBER

pre-math   arts/crafts   object lesson   our world   paper-work

Objective: to study a picture that is not immedi-

ately obvious and to practice seeing and identifying numbers.
Materials needed: crayons and the activity sheet (p. 81).

While you are working on the color by number picture, talk about how God knows what picture he is making out of our lives even when it might not be visible to us. Discernment means trying to see things as God does. Be looking all the time you work for clues that would indicate what the drawing is going to be. What community helper is pictured?

BEAN BAGS

game   word concepts   physical activity

Objective: to review the Bible story and the concepts empty and full.
Materials needed: a sock, string, and beans.

Based on the story of Joseph filling his brother's sacks with grain and legumes, fill a sock with beans. Review the story. Decide whether the sock is empty or full. Tie the open end with string and use the sock as a bean bag. Play hot potato, balance it on your head, try to throw it into a pot from behind a line, etc.

WEEK THREE

BIGGER BARNS

story   object lesson

Objective: to show that discernment means planning for heavenly treasures.
Materials needed: a handful of change and a few pieces of jewelry.

Tell your child you will be talking about treasure. Let him look at and finger the little hoard you have brought together. Ask him if he thinks you'll be able to take it with you when you die. Use that as a springboard for the story that originates in Luke 12:16-24.

There once was a man who was very rich. He had many fields and many flocks. At the end of the harvest, he had so many goods, he didn't even have any place to put it all. So he decided to tear down his old barns and put up newer, better, and bigger storehouses. Then he could put away all the things that he had and live happily ever after.

Perhaps he sat in a rocker on the front porch with his feet up and a glass of lemonade in his hand thinking about all the things he was storing away. We do know for sure that he said to himself, "Self, you have enough stuff saved up to last for many years. Why don't you take it easy, relax, eat all you want, drink all you want, and have a grand old time?"

But God had another name for this pathetic old guy who didn't have an ounce of discernment. He called him a fool. "Fool," the Lord said, "you are going to die tonight. Then what's going to happen to all the riches that you have so carefully hoarded away?" The man had totally forgotten to save up treasures in heaven!

SPORTS NUT

Objective: to introduce several different sports.

Recall the story of the man who built up earthly riches, then relaxed and said, "Now I can play and do whatever I want." He never got to enjoy his playtime because he was so foolish with his work time.

What kinds of things can people do for play? Choose a couple of your favorite sports and play a modified version of them. Use a stick to knock a small ball into a cup for golf. Or throw a ball between your legs and kick it across a yard to make a hike and punt as in

football. Or arrange some obstacles for hurdles and see how far you can jump in a track meet setup.

WHICH IS BIGGER?

Objective: to compare items using _____, _____er, _____est.

Look for things around the house to use for comparison. Use (1) big, bigger, biggest (like the man with the barns); (2) dark, darker, darkest; (3) sharp, sharper, sharpest; (4) quick, quicker, quickest; (5) messy, messier, messiest; (6) wide, wider, widest; (7) loud, louder, loudest; and (8) soft, softer, softest.

CARROMS

Objective: to provide a game (to go along with the recreation idea mentioned in the story) to number and score.

Materials needed: cups, bowls, masking tape, and coins.

Make a table top into a carrom board. Place several obstacles in the center of the table (cups and bowls). With tape, outline a section of each corner to serve as a goal. You can have two to four players. Give each player ten coins. One player will have all nickels, one all pennies, etc. Assign each player with his playing pieces to a different side of the table. The point of the game is to take turns flicking with your finger all ten coins into one of the goals at the opposite end of the table from where you are sitting. As soon as this is achieved, the round is over. If a coin flies off the table, place it back on the edge from which it fell. Score one point for each one of your coins that lands in a goal at the end of a round. Each game contains four rounds. Let your child keep a running tally of the score.

HIDDEN LETTERS

reading   activity

Objective: to further enforce the thought that discernment means taking a second look to see what is really there.

Look for letters of the alphabet formed by what you see around the house. Take a second look at the bars on the back of a chair to discern a *T* formation. Or study a cupboard door to find the letter *H*. Or notice the letter *O* formed by a doorknob. Try to find as many letters as you can.

WEEK FOUR

UGLY DUCKLING

story

Objective: to realize that discernment means seeing the best in other people despite outward appearances.

Read the following story and enquire how your child would have felt to be the duck that everyone mocked. Does your child ever tease or make fun of anyone else? Does he ever allow outward differences to affect how friendly he is with other people? Does he ever exclude anyone during play?

Cra-a-ack! Mother Duck smiled in relief. The last duckling had finally hatched from the egg. Already the first little ones were cheeping for tasty bugs and grubs. She looked lovingly over her little brood. They were so cute with their yellow, downy feathers all fluffed and their bright little eyes looking up expectantly. Only one of them looked a bit strange, but he'd be all right by evening.

As the days went by, the odd little bird seemed to look more and more peculiar. For one thing, he was always hungry. Already he was bigger and more clumsy than the other ducklings. As for his feathers, well, they were the muddiest color gray the mother duck had ever seen. What was wrong with her child?

His brothers and sisters were growing downright mean. "Look at us," they would say. "We are cuddly and smooth. But you—you are rough and ugly." Then they would chant as they kicked and pecked at him, "Ugly duckling, ugly duckling!" The mother duck just watched with a confused expression as if she didn't know what to think.

Finally, the poor rejected duckling had to leave the rest of the family. Could a bird so tender and young make it on his own? All through the winter, he huddled cold and shivering among the branches of the trees that bent over the lake, but somehow when spring finally arrived, the duckling was still alive.

On the first clear day after the melting snows, the duckling ventured down to the lake for a swim. Just at the water's edge, he heard a mother deer speaking to her little fawn. "Look over there," she was saying with pleasure, "do you see the beautiful swan?" The ugly duckling looked all around. He wanted to see the beautiful swan too. As he was craning his neck to figure out where it had gone, he happened to glance down into the water. When he saw his own reflection, he gasped in surprise. He was the swan they were talking about! His feathers were lovely and white and his neck was long and shapely.

The other ducklings had never discerned that he was not a duck like them at all. How surprised they would be to see the majestic creature he had become!

THING A THONG

story   drama

Objective: to show that the only one who loses when you put other people down is yourself.
Materials needed: three puppets or stuffed animals.

Perform the following puppet script. At the end, have the puppet with the lisp teach the willing one a song that is familiar to your child. Show that they have become fast friends. End with the two puppets giving each other a big hug.

First Puppet: I jutht learned a new thong. Would you like to hear me thing the new thong?

Second Puppet: What's a thong? Don't you mean a song? I know what a song is.

First Puppet: Thath what I thaid. A thong. Anyway, it goeth like thith…

Second Puppet: You talk funny. You don't say your words right. I only like to hear songs when people do them correctly.

First Puppet: Well, I'm trying and I have thith fabulouth thong that I jutht learned and I know you'd like to hear it, tho if you'd jutht be thilent long enough for me to thpeak, I could teach it to you.

Second Puppet: Thpeak! Ha, ha, ha! Did you hear what she said? She said thpeak. What a stupid kid. She can't even pronounce the simplest word. (Puppet #2 leaves laughing and mocking.)

First Puppet: Oh, I'm tho thorry he left. I really wanted him to hear thith wonder thong. It wath all about friendth and having happy timeth. I gueth I'll have to find thomeone elth to thing it to. (Third Puppet pops up) Oh, greetingth. Would you like to hear my thong? We could be friendth if you like.

Third Puppet: Sure, I'd love to hear the song and be your friend.

SMOOTH AS SILK

concepts

math

activity

Objective: to further an understanding of the concept of *rough* and *smooth*.

See how long it takes your child to find and touch something *smooth*. Give the directions and count out loud like a verbal stopwatch until your child performs the task. Then have him find and touch something *rough*. See if he can beat his own time. Continue the contest by switching off between the two directions and counting out each second. The longer you play, the more your child will be forced to search farther afield and more intently for rough or smooth surfaces. Remind him about the swan that started out looking rough and shabby but grew sleek and smooth.

NAP WRITING

reading

concepts

Objective: to afford another chance to practice writing numbers.

Find a rug, blanket, sofa, or sweater which has wool or fur that can be brushed in a distinct direction. With your finger, form numbers in the texture of the surface. As you draw your fingers in the opposite direction of the nap, it will make a variation in the shade of the color so you can see what you have written. Is it rough or smooth?

DISCERNING WHAT GOD SEES

music
activity

Objective: to ingrain a principle through the repetition of a fun song.

Material Needed: activity sheet (p. 83).

Learn the following song (based on the tune of "The Little Dutch Girl") with accompanying hand claps. Don't expect your child to catch on immediately. It may take several days of practice off and on, but once he catches on to the idea, he'll want to sing it all the time.

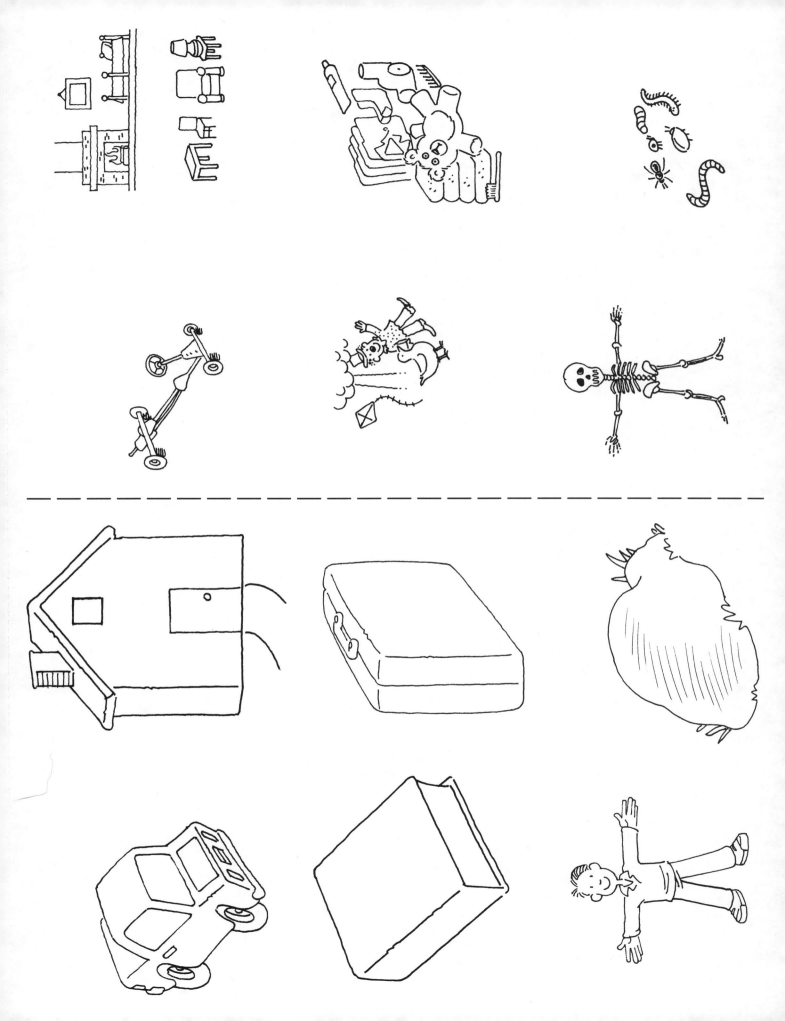

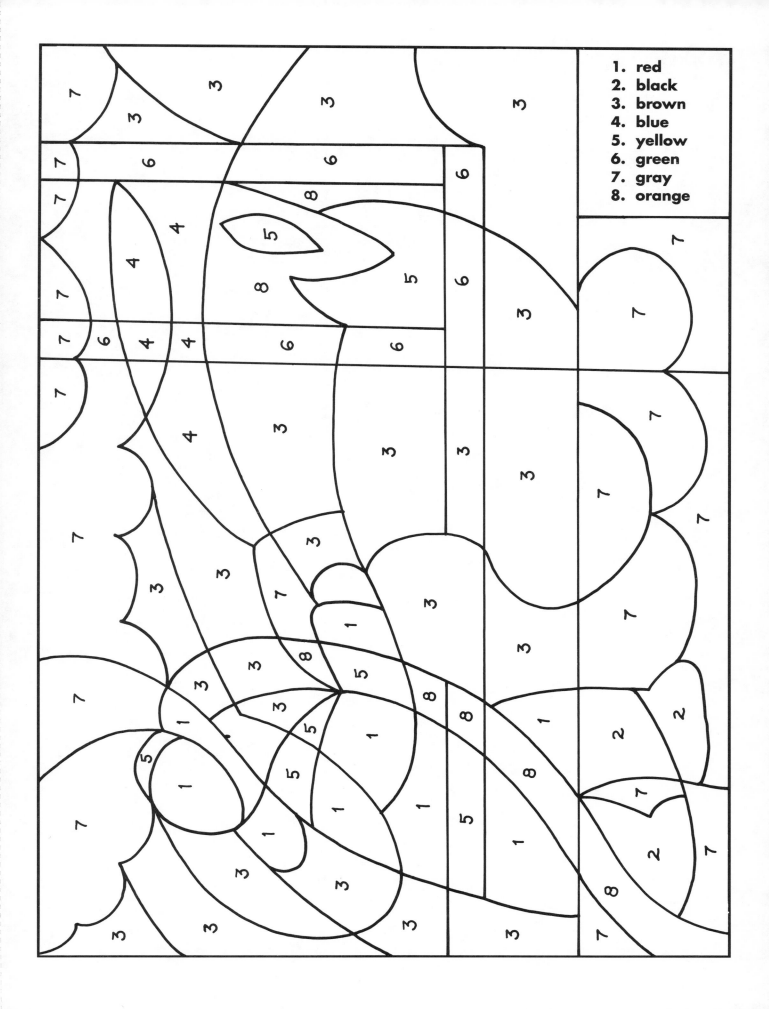

1. red
2. black
3. brown
4. blue
5. yellow
6. green
7. gray
8. orange

I ought to love all peo-ple

no mat - ter who they are

for I have one who loved me when

I strayed so ver - y far.

(clap own hands)

(clap right hand with partner)

(clap own hands)

(clap left hand with partner)

(clap own hand)

(clap both hands with partner)

(clap both hands with partner)

(clap both hands with partner)

Parent and child sit facing each other.

MAY
WEEK ONE

PATIENCE FOR THE PROMISE

story   object lesson

Objective: to show your child that God will perform things in his own time.

Before telling the following story (found in Genesis 12–15), promise your little one that after the lesson, you will give him a snack. Place it on the table where he can see it. If your child becomes impatient and wants the snack right away, use that as a tie-in to the story about Abram who was also promised something but had to believe and patiently wait until God did just what He said.

The men shook their heads in disbelief. What a fool that Abram was! To say that God had told him to move. Move away from everyone and everything that was familiar. And not even to know where he was going. That was the weirdest part. How could you go somewhere when you did not even know where it was?

Abram gave a last pat to the bag that was strapped on the camel's back. He turned around to tell his friends good-bye. "Are you sure you know what you are doing?" they asked. Abram just waved and started down the road with his sheep and other belongings trailing behind him.

It was not an easy trip. Should he turn to the right or to the left? Should he head east or west? Abram had to listen carefully to the voice of God. Many times he probably thought about turning around and going back. But he always remembered the promise of God: "I will take you to a land. It will be your land and the land of your children forever."

After a long journey, he finally arrived at the promised land. But there were already other families living in it. There were short people and tall people working in their houses and fields. There were skinny cows and fat cows grazing in the pastures. There were little gardens and big gardens carefully tended and full of produce. There were old buildings and new buildings sheltering the people from the wind and cold. There were small towns and large towns, teeming with life.

But that didn't matter to Abram. He was discerning enough to know that God would keep His promise anyway and give him a country that would be all his own, even if his old neighbors at home were still shaking their heads.

HOME SWEET HOME

arts/crafts   our world

Objective: to think about what home means and how much Abram would have longed for it.

Materials needed: ribbon or yarn, hole punch, glue, a full-sized paper plate, watercolors, paintbrush, and the activity sheet (p. 93).

Do a little craft by following the instructions on the activity sheet. Talk about your favorite things to do at home.

HOME IS WHERE YOUR HEART IS

word concepts   our world   arts/crafts   paper-work

Objective: to identify *short* and *tall*.

Materials needed: Marking pens and the activity sheet (p. 95).

Look at the different types of homes. Contrast the *short* and *tall* ones. Do you know anyone who lives in any of these kinds of houses? Draw a picture of that person standing outside of his own home. Where would you like to live? Why?

HEAVENLY HOME

Objective: to put your child in Abram's place and show how patiently he waited for the promise.

Materials needed: a blanket and a rope.

Tie the rope between two chairs and throw some blankets over the top, weighted on each corner with a heavy object. Lie on pillows inside the tent and discuss how hard it would be to live in a cloth house all the time. How would you cook? Where would you go to the bathroom? What would you do when the weather turned cold? Show that just as Abram patiently lived in tents waiting for the permanent home God promised, so we live in temporary places on earth patiently waiting for the forever home He's promised in heaven.

HOUSEHOLD OBJECTS

Objective: to use the home as a base for learning about ending sounds.

Materials needed: four paper bags and markers.

Label each bag with one of the following letters: *L*, *K*, *D*, and *R*. Set before your child a variety of items from your household, each one ending with the sound of one of these letters. Some examples would be: pencil, ball, doll, cake, sock, tack, lid, pad, rod, flower, mirror, and pear. Help your child to hear the ending sound; then associate it with the proper letter by placing the object into the correct bag.

READING MINDS

Objective: to show that discernment comes from God.

Have your child pick a number between one and ten. Let him write the number secretly on a piece of paper while you think very hard and try to read his mind. Guess a number. Chances are you'll be wrong. (If you were right, guess again until you miss!) Let your child try the same with you. Use this exercise to prove that only God can read minds. People certainly can't. Move right into the following story taken from Luke 5.

The bright sunlight suddenly streamed into the dark room from above. The people strained forward and stared up through a hole while great blocks of ceiling were removed by the strong hands of four men on the roof. Finally, the work stopped and the dust settled. The people in the room below brushed chunks of plaster from their hair and waited to see what would happen next. They didn't have to wait very long. Something was being lowered through the hole. It was a man in a blanket! The people moved back to let the makeshift bed come to rest in the center of the room. The sick man in the middle blinked up at the crowds staring down at him. Then he shifted his gaze to look into the face of the One he had come to see. Jesus!

Jesus was amazed at everything the sick man and his friends had done to get to Him. And He could see or "discern" what the man wanted most in his heart. He wanted to have the acceptance of God. So Jesus gently told him, "Your sins are forgiven." This was the most wonderful thing that could ever happen to the sick man.

But some bad people in the crowd started

thinking evil thoughts in their hearts. They said to themselves, "Who does Jesus think He is? Only a big-shot would say to anyone that his sins are forgiven!"

But Jesus could see or "discern" what these people were thinking as well. So just to prove that He could do as great a miracle as forgiving sins, He told the man to pick up his bed and walk. Without hesitation, the man stood right up and folded his blanket. With the friends that brought him, he joyfully headed home, praising God all the way.

CAN GOD SEE ME?

Objective: to show that God is aware of everything.

Hide with your child in all the best hiding places around your house. As you crouch in the darkness at each point, ask the question, "Does God know where you are right now?" With this introduction, briefly present a little Gospel message. Begin with the query, if God saw you in all of those places, can He even see inside of you? Does He know when you do something wrong? How does He feel about your sin? What has He done to take care of it? What did He do with the sick man's sin? How can you have the same thing happen to your sin? To prepare yourself for the answers to this series of questions, read John 3.

TAKE UP YOUR BED

Objective: to see *high* and *low* acted out within the framework of the Bible story.
Materials needed: a small piece of material, crayons, scissors, string, and the activity sheet (p. 97).

Follow the instructions on the activity page. Relive the story with an emphasis on the words *high* (when the men were just dropping the pallet through the opening in the roof) and *low* (when it was placed at the feet of our Lord).

HAIRS OF YOUR HEAD

Objective: to see how closely and intimately God knows us.
Materials needed: paper and crayons or markers.

Have your child draw a fairly complete picture of himself. Starting at the feet, have your child state and write on the page the numbers that apply to each body part (i.e., 2 hands, 10 fingers, 1 mouth, etc.). When you get to hair, have him count the number of hairs he drew. Is that accurate? Have him count the actual hairs on his head. He can't? Then remind him that God knows everything about him, including how many hairs are on his head. How's that for discernment!

PERFECT PITCH

Objective: to hear the difference between high and low sounds.

Sing a note and encourage your child to match it with his own voice. Indicate with your thumb whether the note he is singing ought to be higher or lower. After he catches the right pitch, sing another note and let him try to match it again. Remind him of the highs and lows of the man's bed in the Bible story.

WEEK THREE

FALSE ADVERTISING

drama   world

Objective: to help your child learn the fallacies in the world of advertising.

Dress up in a crazy hat or tie like a slick salesperson. Pick an item to sell to your child. Place it on the table between you and your youngster and use every gimmick you can to convince him that he ought to have it. Make some outlandish claims. Tell him it is a bargain that he will never again get a chance to have. Appeal to everything that is attractive. Make your child believe that he cannot live without this item. After you have finished your sales pitch, remove the costume and talk about what you did. Was everything you said really true? Was it really the deal it appeared to be? Could your youngster get along without it?

All the children dropped their toys, left their chores, and ran as fast as their bare feet could carry them through the dusty streets of town. It was a hot day in summer during one of the early years of our country.

"The peddler's cart has arrived!" William shouted at his buddy James through the open door of his father's carpentry shop.

James' eyes pleaded with his father as he brushed the sawdust from his work apron. "Pa," he asked anxiously, "may I go with William? I won't be gone long!"

The tall man with the big muscles in his arms paused in his work to smile at his son. "You may go," he said to James. "But I'll need you in a little bit to finish this order of chairs by evening." James hardly waited for the last of his father's words. He was out the door and down the street almost before he laid down his tools.

The peddler had already begun his speech by the time James and William joined the small crowd of townspeople. He was standing on a wooden box right by the side of his colorful wagon. "Ladies and Gentlemen!" he shouted. "I have here the most remarkable stuff ever invented by man." He held a small brown bottle high in the air for everyone to see.

James was having a good time. He loved to watch the little man with his puffy red cheeks. He liked to hear the peddler tell about what he had to sell.

"Yes, sir!" the peddler continued in a booming voice. "No matter what your problem, my product here will completely take care of it. If you have a stomachache, a teaspoonful will make you totally well. If you spill your dinner on your shirt, just a few drops will remove the stain. It will produce blossoms on plants, clean dirty pots, and soothe tired feet. Step right up and buy some today."

James and William looked at each other and laughed. How could anybody believe all those things? James and William would not be fooled. Their parents had taught them to be wise and discerning.

Suddenly from the crowd, a man waved a fist in anger. "I bought one of your little brown bottles when you were last in town," he shouted. "It didn't do anything you said it would."

"So did I," said a sweet-faced woman who stood near the front. "I don't think you are telling the truth."

James wished he could stay and see what would happen next, but he had to get back to his father's shop. One way or another, he had a feeling that peddler was in for a hard time.

ADS COLLAGE

arts/crafts   world

Objective: to help your child look through a magazine without wishing for everything that he sees.

Materials needed: a toy catalog or a magazine with a lot of ads, construction paper, scissors, and glue.

Look at advertisements and let your child tear out the ones that appeal to him. Glue them together on a page to create a collage. After you've finished, study the pictures to see how the ads make the item for sale seem more wonderful than it really is. What are some of the tricks the advertisers used?

DISCERNING VALUE

Objective: to learn to identify that which is *cheap* and that which is more *valuable*.

Take a close look for comparison at the difference between two similar items, one that is *cheaply* made and one that is well-made. Compare two pieces of furniture, items of clothing, pieces of jewelry, etc. Look at craftsmanship and materials. Instill an appreciation of *value*.

MEDIA MATH

Objective: to use the media to identify numbers.

Materials needed: a radio or television.

Show your child how to turn the dial or program the remote control to change stations on the radio or TV. Call out numbers and let him find the channel that corresponds. Review your rules for watching and listening. Renew your commitment to high standards of Christ-honoring programming.

DISCERNING GOD'S CALL

Objective: to contrast the world's view of failure with God's view of success.

Materials needed: a broom, old clothing, construction paper, masking tape, and scissors.

Dress up a broom to be a handicapped or invalid woman. Make facial features out of the construction paper and tape them onto the straw. Tie a scarf around her head, and lay her down on a bed. Introduce her to your child. Pretend that the broom lady apologizes to the child for not getting up to meet him but explains that she is confined to bed. Carry on a lively conversation. Make it clear that although the world would consider her useless, she enjoys life to the fullest. Does she lie around all day and watch TV and just wish that she could be up? Oh, no! She is far too busy for empty television shows and discontented wishing. She spends her time praying for missionaries, knitting blankets for the poor, writing letters to elected officials, singing to the Lord, and visiting with all the wonderful people God brings to her—like your child.

WEEK FOUR

HOT STUFF

Objective: to point out that discernment means knowing when to stand alone for the right.

Sit facing each other. Tell your child to sit when you sit and stand when you stand. Try to throw him off by an unanticipated movement or by only half sitting when he expects you to go all the way. Then tell the story of the three men and the fiery furnace found in

Daniel 3. How did these men stand alone?

The king was furious. How dare those impertinent young men refuse to bow down to the statue of himself! He would give them only one more chance. Perhaps they had misunderstood the instructions.

"Listen carefully," the king exploded. "If you do not worship the golden statue that I have made, I will immediately throw you into a burning hot furnace. Do you understand now?"

It did not matter to the three boys that they were the only people in the whole land who refused to bow down to the image. And it did not matter that the king said he would throw them into a fiery furnace. They were discerning enough to decide what was right and to stand up for it.

When the music began to signal the people to bow down in front of the statue once more, the king looked directly at the young men to see what they would do. Straight and tall they stood without flinching even a little bit. In a rage, the king commanded his servants to bind the boys and throw them into the furnace. It was so scorching hot that the men throwing them in died on the spot.

After a while, the fire began to burn itself out. The king came close to see if there was anything left but ashes. There in the middle of the furnace, walking around in the last of the embers, were all three boys with an angel of the Lord beside them.

The king finally began to discern his own stupidity. He admitted that the young men had actually been right all along.

DISCERNING CHOICES

Objective: to give real life examples of times to stand alone.
Materials needed: a writing utensil and the activity sheet (p. 99).

Look carefully at the illustrations. Set them up for your child to put himself into the action. How could he or she stand alone for what is right in each of these situations?

COLD FEET

Objective: to find out where to experience the sensation of *hot* and *cold* and to identify those simple words.
Materials needed: paper and pencil, tape, and scissors.

Print the words *hot* and *cold* three times each on separate pieces of paper. Secure them with tape so they can stick like labels around the house. With your child, study the letters and the sounds they make to learn the two words. Look together for places you know that are traditionally *hot*, like stoves, furnaces, fireplaces, and irons. Help your child attach the labels to a safe place on or near the items. Do the same with the *cold* labels for things such as refrigerators, freezers, basements, and back porches.

NO, I WON'T!

Objective: to prepare your child for specific instances where discernment would advise him to say "no."

Prompt your child to learn these words and say them firmly, "No, I won't!" Set up particular situations and have him practice the desired response by standing to his feet and repeating the phrase with enthusiasm.

(1) A friend says, "Stay a little longer at the park. Your dad is too busy to notice you're a little late."

(2) A stranger says, "Come with me and take a ride in my car."

(3) A cousin says, "Try a little smoke.

Everyone's into it and it makes you really cool."

(4) A sister says, "Let's have some candy from the cupboard. No one will see us."

(5) A kid from the church says, "I'll race you up the aisle of the auditorium. Ready, set, go."

(6) A neighbor says, "Show me your private place. You don't have to tell your parents."

(7) A kid on the block says, "Let's go down the street to my friend's house. He has a neat toy. Just tell your mom you were at my house."

(8) A brother says, "Help me glue this lamp back together. Please don't get me in trouble with Mom.

SHIVER OR SWEAT

word concepts   skill   physical activity

Objective: to contrast hot and cold drinks.

Materials needed: apple juice, ice cubes, and cloves.

Fix a mug of hot apple cider and a frosty glass of cold apple juice. Note the difference in feel and taste. Which better suits the type of weather you are experiencing today? What kind of weather would be better for the drink that you did not select? Would the three men in the Bible story have felt hot or cold when standing in the fiery furnace? If they were thirsty, which drink would they have preferred?

1. Have your child paint the picture.

2. While it dries, take a paper plate and hole-punch at regular intervals around the edge.

3. Let your child thread yarn in and out of the holes and tie a bow at the top. The yarn will go through the holes much easier if the end is dipped in fingernail polish, then allowed to harden.

4. Cut out the circle on this page and mount it on the front of the paper plate.

Do you know anybody who lives in a home like any of these? Draw the person standing beside the place he or she lives.

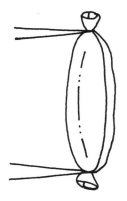

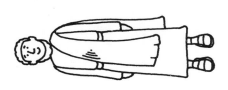

1. Mount the figure on a construction paper background. Cut him out.

2. Tie a piece of material with string at both ends to form a bed.

3. Place the sick man on his bed, ready to be carried by friends to meet Jesus— or–sling the bed over his shoulder in response to Jesus' command to "pick up your bed and walk."

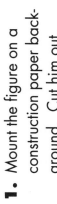

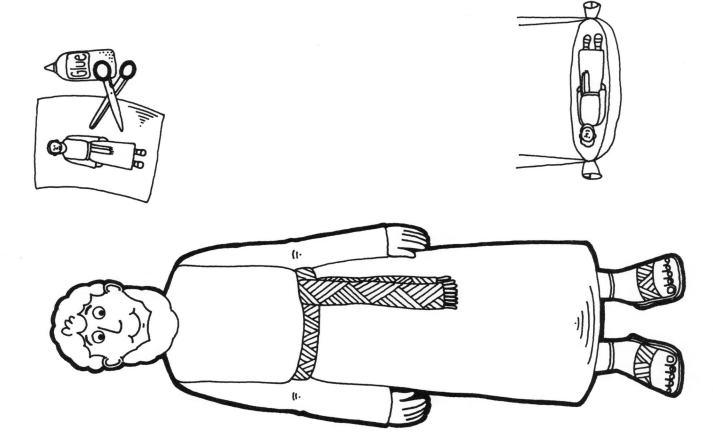

SUMMER

INTRODUCTION

The people of Israel prospered tremendously under the reign of King David. They experienced freedom from the terror of enemies because of the courage and expertise of David's defending army. They enjoyed a measure of economic success and financial freedom because David did not tax exorbitantly as did other rulers of his day. They were encouraged to seek after and serve the Lord because David as their leader had a heart that was eager to know God.

But in spite of his achievements, in the lat-

ter years of his reign, there were several men who attempted to usurp David's authority and throne. One was a cocky young man by the name of Adonijah. First, he declared himself king. Then he had the nerve to hire fifty chariots, horsemen, and runners to precede his entry into the capital and arrange a coup and proclaim a change of leadership.

Who was this anarchist? A rookie army captain whose few, incidental victories had gone to his head? An ignorant foreigner who was unaware of the satisfaction of Israel's citizenship and thought he could drum up a backing of disgruntles? A tender novice from David's own court who had been hurt or offended by a careless word from the king? No. The rebel was none other than David's own son! Why did he do this terrible thing against his own father?

We have a clue when the Bible states that during all the years of Adonijah's adolescence, David never once crossed his son's will or questioned anything he did. So because of the indulgence of his father, Adonijah was raised a spoiled brat and when he was grown, he turned into a radical and antagonistic revolutionary.

Where do you draw the lines in your own family? Have you decided what actions or attitudes are worthy of discipline? What requires a creative character building assignment, and what demands the infliction of physical punishment? If both parents are present when a child breaks a rule, who will act? If parents disagree over the crime and punishment, what then? When correction is invoked and there is no repentance, is there another step? Parents must discuss these issues and decide on guidelines before incidents occur. Then they must mediate with promptness, consistency, and love.

Look at this sampling of verses from Scripture and note that the teaching is quite informative and comprehensive concerning the subject of discipline. We start with the basics and progress to the more complex issues involved in the correction process.

(1) Proverbs 3:12; 13:24. If parents truly love their child, they will correct him.

(2) Job 5:17. Children are actually happier within the boundaries of discipline.

(3) Proverbs 15:5; 29:15. The result of reproof is instruction and wisdom. The result of negligence is shameful behavior.

(4) Proverbs 23:13-14. Punishment will not physically kill your child, but withholding it will spiritually kill him.

(5) Hebrews 12:9. Discipline promotes a reverence for all authority and an ability to submit to the powers that be.

(6) Jeremiah 10:24. Punishment should only be administered in love. Disciplining in anger will destroy a child.

(7) Jeremiah 5:3. Discipline (if properly applied and received) should affect the mind, will, and emotions.

(8) 2 Timothy 3:16. It is both appropriate and prudent to use Scripture as part of the correction process.

(9) Proverbs 19:18. Crying is not necessarily an indication that punishment has done what it was supposed to do.

(10) Isaiah 26:16. The proper response of the child to correction is to submit himself to the will of the parent and to fall upon his mercy.

(11) Psalm 73:14. Discipline requires consistency. You cannot let up when tired or inconvenienced. If you do, you establish the precedent that there are certain times when it is acceptable to be disrespectful and disobedient.

(12) Psalm 94:10; James 1:5. God has perfect knowledge of your child's heart and what he really deserves. We can go to God for wisdom when we're not sure how to act in any disciplinary situation.

(13) 1 Kings 12:11-16. Be sensitive to God's leading so that you might stop correction before it becomes excessive or oppressive.

(14) Deuteronomy 11:2; Isaiah 17:7-9. Part of comprehending God's greatness and strength is understanding the justice of His judgments; therefore, our authority and influence is established in the eyes of our children by the fairness and equity of the chastisements we give.

(15) Luke 23:16, 23. How your child responds to affliction is entirely up to him. God provides the grace for him to react with a sweet and happy spirit even if we as parents make an honest mistake in judgment.

(16) Hebrews 12:7-8; Matthew 18:15-17. It is not up to us to correct the children of another family. However, there might come an extreme time to hold an offending one

accountable before elders and let them deal with a situation.

For every negative trait you attempt to counter, there is always a corresponding positive characteristic to instill. For example, while you combat the problem of ingratitude, you must also encourage the quality of thankfulness. While you seek to discourage selfishness, you must be looking for ways for your child to express love. Correction always works hand in hand with instruction.

How can a parent encourage spiritual sensitivity to both teaching and reproof? Is there an ingredient that can stir up a heart that is fresh and impressionable when it comes to the things of the Lord? Is it possible for a parent to keep a child's conscience from being seared? Can we develop a receptivity in our little one's heart to the promptings of the Holy Spirit?

There are three illustrations from Scripture that show a parent how to keep the doors of his children's spiritual receptivity swung open wide. The first is found in Ephesians 3:17-19. This passage seems to suggest that spiritual comprehension and an alertness to the things of God come as a natural result of being rooted and grounded in the faith. When a plant establishes itself in the soil, it derives nourishment and stability from the ground in which it is planted. The more we integrate our children's everyday experiences with the Word of God, the more they will rely on God for what they need and become unshaken in their scriptural outlook.

John 10:27 provides a second picture. Believers are like sheep who follow the Shepherd. They instinctively run after the voice they recognize. The more familiar our children are with Scripture, the easier it will be for them to perceive and follow Christ's voice.

The last example is found in Hebrews 5:14. This verse states that a steady diet on the meat of the Bible will over time produce a person who can automatically distinguish between good and bad. Isn't that exactly what we want?

So using the pictures of the plant thrusting its roots deep into the soil, a sheep trotting happily along the path of his beloved shepherd, and a man pushing aside a plate of garbage to take up a delicious and wholesome meal, Scripture attempts to illustrate a common point. The more we derive our life and teachings from the Word of God, the easier it will be for our children to respond to the guidance and direction of the Lord.

On the one hand, we can easily become overwhelmed by all of the contrary behavior and the negative traits we wish we could change. On the other hand, we can plead for wisdom in establishing within our children an indigenous desire to know God. Discipline will deliver the knockout punch to the sin in their lives, and character building activities will offer a hand to pull them back up. What a victory it will be when we, as trainers, can hold up the arms of our children like champions in the ring. How thrilling to present them before God as triumphant winners!

JUNE
WEEK ONE

NOAH'S ARK

story   object lesson

Objective: to illustrate that obedience provides safety.
Materials needed: animal toys and a large bowl.

Set out the bowl and as many different animal toys as you can collect. Tell the story of Noah as recorded in Genesis 7. When you get to the part about the animals coming into the ark, let your child march each one into the safety of the bowl-boat.

"Bang, bang." The hammer in Noah's hand beat in steady rhythm as he followed the last of God's instructions for building the big boat. His three sons were helping to put tar on the sides, fit the door into place, and complete the roof. It was not an easy job.

Finally they put the finishing touches on the huge ark. The neighbors could not understand it at all. They mocked, "We are miles away from the sea. And even if there was a way to move it, your boat is so big it would never float!" They poked one another in the ribs and laughed loudly. But Noah and his sons did not listen. As the last board fit snugly into place, they felt happy to know that they had obeyed God's commands to the best of their ability.

When Noah and his sons were done, and the animals could come by pairs into the ship. There were birds and creepy-crawly things, cuddly animals, and ferocious beasts. Noah made a spot for each one. As soon as the last of the creatures was on board, God shut the great door. Almost immediately, the rain began to pour. Water cascaded from the sky, and the oceans emptied themselves onto the land. But Noah didn't have a worry in the world because he had listened and obeyed.

Now God was taking care of him.

At last one morning, it was quiet. The rain stopped its pounding on the roof and the boat rocked gently back and forth. Days later it would land on a mountain, and Noah and his family would open the door and be free to live on the earth once more.

VEHICLES

world   arts/crafts

Objective: to consider the many different kinds of transportation vehicles in the world.
Materials needed: a large box, markers, construction paper, and glue.

Remember the story about Noah's big ship. What are some other vehicles? (Define a vehicle as the means to get from one place to another.) Work on constructing a car, plane, boat, bus, train, etc. out of the cardboard box by adding steering wheels, rudders, wings, propellers, tires, or whatever amenities apply. Would Noah have had an easy time building his craft? Think how he obeyed even when it was hard.

SUNK BUT DRY

concepts   science   activity

Objective: to visualize the difference between *sinking* and *floating*.
Materials needed: a cup and a paper towel

Perform a little magic trick in a tub of water. Stuff a dry paper towel into the bottom of a cup. Submerge the cup, rim straight down into the water. Let the water completely cover the cup. If the cup is not tipped, the paper towel will remain dry because of the air trapped inside! After your child has had a chance to perfect and perform the trick for himself, check out the materials you are using. Do they *sink* or *float*? Think about Noah and his boat. Did it sink or float?

UP, UP IN THE AIR

Objective: to recognize another method of locomotion and to identify number sequences.

Materials needed: activity sheet (p. 111) and a pencil.

Follow the dots to see yet another transportation vehicle. What makes it go? What would you see from up there? Is it fast? Would your child like to ride in one? Would he like to have been in the ark with Noah? Why or why not?

ROLL 'EM

Objective: to demonstrate the importance of wheels on heavy moving vehicles.

Materials needed: as many wheeled vehicles as you can muster from around the house.

Do an experiment. Lay wagons, trikes, wheelbarrows, etc. on their sides. Is it very easy to pull or push them along? Put them upright, resting on their wheels. Now is it any easier to pull or push them along? What is the difference? Where did the ark finally come to rest? (Answer: Mt. Ararat.) Could it have been easily moved once it landed?

W E E K   T W O

PETER'S PLEASURE PLANES

Objective: to learn that responsibility means not neglecting the little things.

Stick out your arms and pretend to be a plane zooming through the air. Wouldn't it be fun to fly? Read the following story about a plane that never even got off the ground.

There was once a small company that made airplanes. The people at this company didn't make great big jetliners to take hundreds of passengers across oceans to far-away places. They did not make fighter planes that flew faster than sound and could shoot at enemy aircraft. However, they were great at making lightweight, little pleasure planes to fly out to the country for a picnic or travel to the beach to dig for clams.

The company was called "Peter's Pleasure Planes" and consisted of two men—Peter (the owner) and his partner Paul. And between the two of them, they made one airplane a year in a great big barn behind Peter's house. They had a schedule to follow each month to keep up with production, so when Paul called in sick for twenty days in November with the chicken pox, Peter was beside himself, worrying how to get everything done. Some nights, Peter would stay at work until after ten with a little light bulb burning brightly overhead while he tried to figure out how to do what Paul usually did when he was there.

Peter was just screwing on the last part of the propeller one morning when he heard Paul's cheery whistle. Wheeling around, he thought he had never seen a more wonderful face than that of his partner's. "I've had a miserable time without you!" Peter said as he gave Paul a tremendous bear hug. "There were so many things I did not know how to do. I needed you here."

Paul turned his attention right away toward the plane. "Why, it looks beautiful," he declared, running his hand gently along a shiny wing. "It looks ready to fly. I don't think there's a thing left for me to do."

"Well, I did the best I could without you," Peter said modestly. "If you like, we can take her up for a test flight." The two men slipped on goggles, flying suits, and matching scarves and pushed the plane out onto the little runway behind the barn.

"Start her up," shouted Peter into the wind. With a cough and a sputter, the little engine began to hum. The propeller spun faster and faster, and it looked as if all systems were go. Just then, both men heard a massive crunch, the plane began to lurch on the ground, and the propeller flew off right into the side of the barn where it stuck like a dart. Then all was quiet.

"What did I do wrong?" wailed Peter. Paul hunched over the motor in deep thought. Then he looked closely and snapped his fingers. "I know just the problem," he stated firmly. "You've left out a very small but important part!" He ran into the barn and came right back with a tiny screw in his hand. Fastening the screw onto the motor with an ever ready screwdriver from his pocket, he tried to explain to Peter how the airplane could not run without it and what might have happened had they been in the air before the engine shut down.

Peter shook his head in disbelief. He had known the screw was supposed to go somewhere, but he hadn't been able to figure out where. And since it was so little, he had decided to leave it out. Sometimes when you have a big responsibility, little things can be very important.

HIGH-POWERED

Objective: to see what kinds of energy makes things go.

Look around the house and garage to find at least one machine that is run by each of the following sources of energy: battery, gasoline, natural gas, sun, and electricity. Take a look at as many of the energy sources as you can: open the back of a battery powered radio, see how a vacuum plugs into the wall, look at the electrical panel on the house, take the gas cap off the lawn mower and look in the tank, study the holes in the coil of the stove through which the natural gas can be released, etc. What made the airplane in the story go?

WHAT'S MISSING?

Objective: to notice a missing element and identify what should be there.
Materials needed: activity sheet (p. 113) and a writing utensil.

Draw in the missing part of the machines and appliances. How well would they work without the missing item? Think together about a task you perform around the house. What would happen if you forgot to do a small but essential part of the job? How important are details?

HIDDEN NUMBERS

Objective: to note number sequences and determine what's missing.
Materials needed: paper, scissors, and pen.

Write a series of numbers on a piece of paper. Take a small square of paper and cover one of the numbers so it is hidden from your child's view. What is the missing number? Repeat with other numbers. How important is each number? If there were no number fours for example, animals would have to walk on three legs, your child would have no birthday the year after three, and we would have no Independence Day celebrations.

HUMAN ENERGY

nature | science | skill | physical | activity

Objective: to see that people use food as an energy source.

Materials needed: craft sticks, ice cube tray, aluminum foil, and fruit juice.

Make popsicles by pouring juice into the ice cube tray. Cover the tray with foil. Place one upright stick into each compartment, poking a hole through the foil. Freeze. As you work on the snack, discuss how moving things are propelled by some kind of energy. Humans get their energy from food. What would happen if you forgot to eat? How important is a small thing like a nutritious breakfast?

WEEK THREE

DO I HAVE TO?

story | world

Objective: to understand the consequences of not following through on a responsibility.

List some of your child's responsibilities and remind him of some of your own. Tell the following story. Does your child ever feel the same way that Matt did? What would happen if your child stopped doing his chores? Name one important responsibility shouldered by each member of the family. Make a commitment to your child that you will do your job to the best of your ability. Urge him to do the same.

"I'm just sick of doing my chores," Matt sighed wearily. The bucket dropped from his hand to the barn floor with a clank, and he scowled at Missy the cat as she rubbed up against his leg and purred. He pushed her away and flopped down against a bale of hay. He watched the dust swirl in the light that streamed through the partly open doors. He hated his jobs! But Missy did not mind if he was in a bad mood and gracefully kneaded his leg and rubbed the sides of her face contentedly against his hand.

It was Matt's job to feed all the animals. What would Missy do without him he wondered as she curled up happily into a ball of fur on his lap? What if he did not put crunchy brown food in her bowl or fill up her container with cool, clean water? What if he did not supply the horse with alfalfa, the pigs with slop, and the chickens with grain?

He imagined the animals—thin, dirty, sick, and crying or bleating for his help. They needed him! He had an important task. He would not let them down!

POP GOES THE WEASEL

music | physical | activity | world

Objective: to put your child in the role of an animal.

Key off the animals in the story about Matt and his jobs. Name some barnyard animals, forest creatures, and jungle wildlife. Which ones depend on us to help them? If you have access to an animal picture book or an encyclopedia, look up monkeys and weasels. Teach the following song. If you are not familiar with the tune, learn it as a poem. Frolic around the room on the first three lines like a monkey with shoulders hunched and knuckles to the floor. On "POP," jump into the air, then fall to the ground.

All around the cobbler's bench,
the monkey chased the weasel.
The monkey thought 'twas all in fun.
POP—goes the weasel!

LION TAMERS

concepts   world   activity

Objective: to understand how much is involved in animal husbandry and to contrast *wild* and *tame.*

Select one *tame* and one *wild* animal. Pretend they are both coming to visit. Prepare a separate place for each of them to stay. Figure out what you will give them to eat and drink. If they need special enclosures, water for swimming, trees for climbing, or other special attention, include them in your plans.

ANIMAL FLASHCARDS

reading   world

Objective: to hear the beginning sound in a few animal names.
Materials needed: index cards and crayons.

In a nice big script, print a letter on one side of an index card. Put different letters on several other cards. Hold the cards up, one at a time, and ask your child to think of an animal that starts with that letter. Use letters like *B, C, E, F,* and *G.* If your child draws a blank, prompt him with a few suggestions like bears, cats, elephants, fish, and goats. Turn each card over and have him draw the corresponding animal on the back. Use as flashcards.

PEAS 'N PICKS ANIMALS

world   crafts

Objective: to give a chance to review the character story and the animal theme.
Materials needed: peas, potatoes, and toothpicks.

Talk about animals and the responsibilities of their owners. What are some other things a person can possess that impart responsibility? Think of babies, vehicles, homes, gardens, etc. What does the person in charge have to do to keep them growing, running, and in order? While you discuss these things, provide the suggested materials to sculpture animals, known and unknown. Stick the peas onto the potato bodies with toothpicks to make features and limbs.

WEEK FOUR

SLOTHS AND SLUGS

crafts   work

Objective: to illustrate the biblical view of a lazy man.
Materials needed: paper and crayons.

Describe the slow meticulous movements of sloths and slugs. Tell how the Bible describes lazy people as "slothful" and "sluggardly." Read the following quotations (taken from *The Living Bible*) and let your child illustrate the verses within a drawing.

Proverbs 26:13-14: "The lazy man...sticks to his bed like a door to its hinges." (Draw a person in bed.)
Proverbs 23:21: "Too much sleep clothes a man with rags." (Put holes in the person's blankets and clothes.)
Proverbs 20:4: "If you won't plow in the cold, you won't eat at the harvest." (Picture an empty cupboard.)
Proverbs 24:30-31: "The field of...a lazy fellow...was covered with weeds and its walls were broken down." (Show a yard through an open window with weeds and broken walls.)
Ecclesiates 10:18: "Laziness lets the roof leak, and soon the rafters begin to rot." (Sketch a leaky roof with rotting rafters.)

THANKS FOR BEING YOU

crafts   skill

Objective: to help your child see his God-given potential.

Materials needed: crayons, glue, scissors, light cardboard, and the activity sheet (p. 115).

Mount the picture on cardboard and let your child color it to look as much like himself as the drawing allows. Cut out the pieces. Help your child to complete the puzzle. While you are working on this project, compliment your child on his strengths. Talk about what makes him special and unique. Suggest some areas to work on. Particularly evaluate how he is doing as a responsible worker. Emphasize how much you love him.

SWIFT SWEEPS

skill   concepts   activity

Objective: to experience *fast* action and contrast it with *slow*.

Materials needed: a whistle and a broom.

Remind your child what God says about sluggards. Is it good to dawdle about your work? On the other hand, should a person do a job so hurriedly that it is not done with care or expertise? Show your child how to sweep with a broom. Take up a whistle. When you blow it once, he should stroke very *slowly;* when you blow it twice, he should work *fast* with quick, brisk movements.

THE FISH ARE BITING

world   math

Objective: to consider the physical features of a human being.

Take a look at your bodies. Ask your child to identify different body parts. Introduce some new terms like *shin, wrist, ankle, jaw, temple,* etc. Teach the following poem by asking him to hold up one finger for each number. When the poem states where the child was bitten, let him point to the appropriate body part.

1, 2, 3, 4, 5; I caught a fish alive.
6, 7, 8, 9, 10; I let him go again.
Why did you let him go? Because he bit my finger so.
Which finger did he bite? The little finger on the right.

FACE PRINTS

world   crafts   activity

Objective: to see that physical features are not the most important part of a person, rather what is most important is what he does with his knowledge.

Materials needed: 2 cups flour, 1 cup salt, 2 cups water, 4 tbs. oil, 1 tsp. food coloring, 4 tsp. cream of tartar, and a saucepan.

Make a batch of playdough. Stir all the ingredients over medium heat until the mixture comes away from the sides of the pan. Knead until cool enough for your child to handle. Roll into a flat round. Place it over the child's face, making holes for eyes and nose. Press against the skin to make an impression. Remove and compare the inverted image with the real shape in the mirror. While you are working together on the project, speak about how a person's looks do not make him who he is. If, for example, your child's face were scarred in some kind of accident, you would love him just the same and he would still be a wonderful person. There is *somebody* inside his skin and bones. If that somebody has become God's child, the inside person can make the outside shell radiant with beauty.

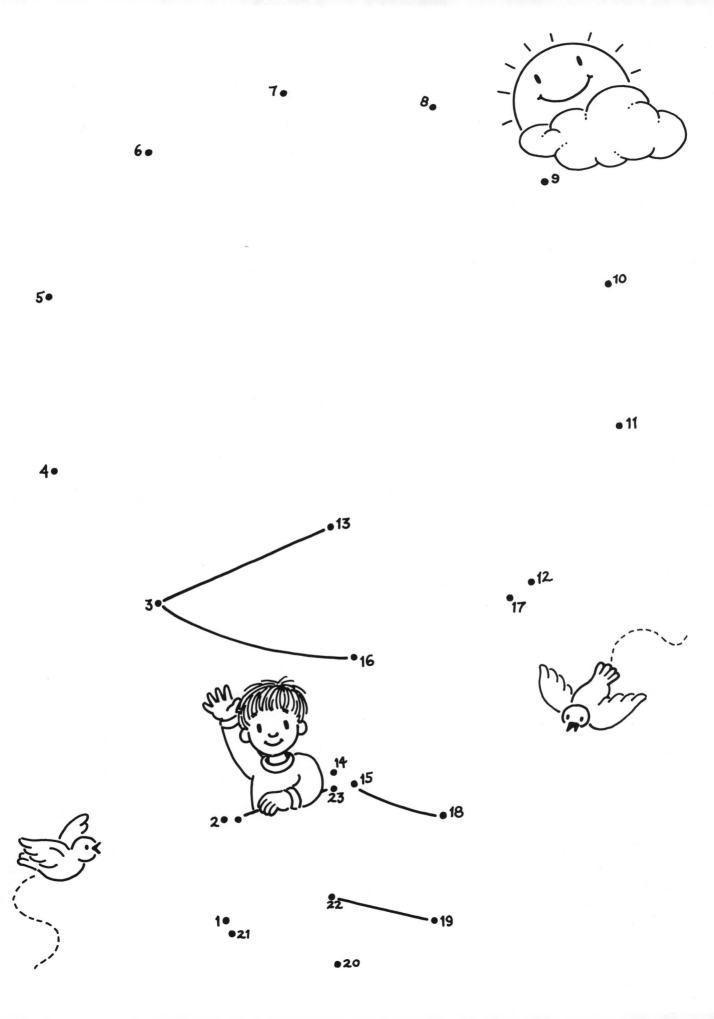

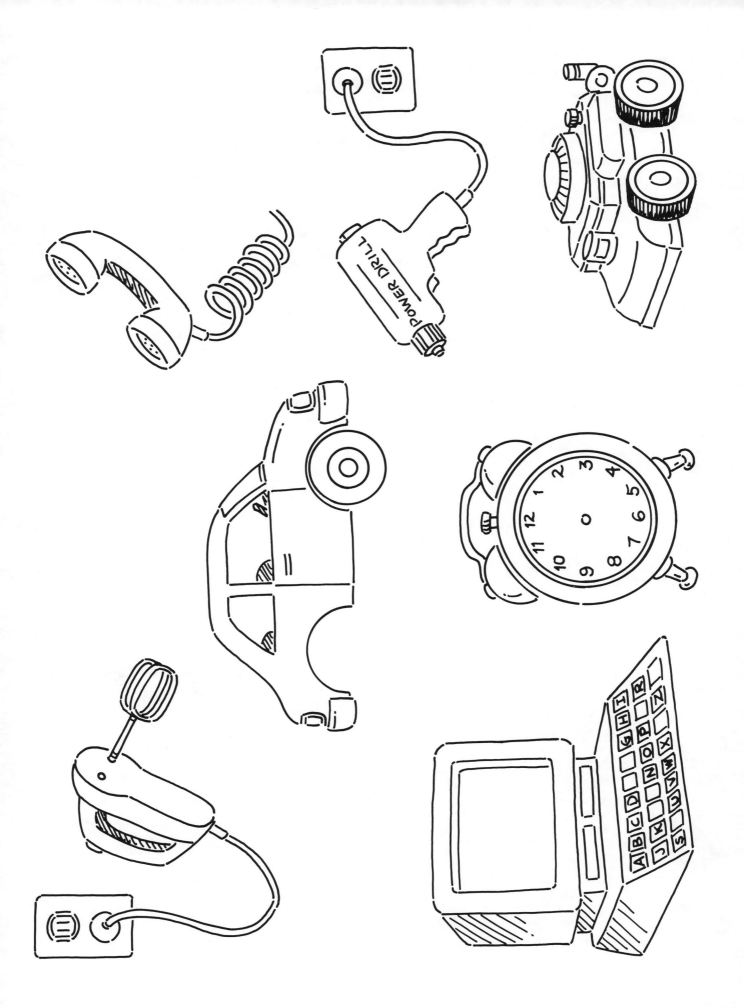

JULY
WEEK ONE

TAKING CARE OF OTHERS

story

drama

Objective: to learn the responsibility involved in watching out for somebody else.

Materials needed: a blanket, soft cloth, glue, scissors, the activity sheet (p. 123), and crayons or colored pencils (optional).

Drape a blanket over the back of a sofa to use as a backdrop. If you desire, lightly color the pictures on the activity sheet. Cut out the figures. Glue small squares of soft cloth on the back of each one. They will now stick to the blanket like flannelgraph figures. Use the pictures to tell the following story from Exodus 32.

"Where's Moses?" the people whined to Aaron. Aaron was Moses' brother. He was in charge now that Moses had gone up the mountain to talk to God. "We're tired of waiting for him to come back," the Children of Israel continued. "We're tired of worshiping a God we are not sure is really there. We want you to make us a god we can see."

Taking care of millions of people would not be an easy job for anybody. Have you ever helped your mom or dad take care of even one little brother or sister? But Aaron knew that worshiping idols was a terrible thing." He should have shown the people how wrong it was.

But Aaron did not realize what an important job he had. He coolly replied, "OK." He asked the people to bring their golden jewelry. He melted it all down and took an engraving tool and formed a calf. Then he told the people that this could be their god.

The whole nation threw a party. They brought presents to the golden calf and sang and prayed to it as if it had been the one to take care of them all this time, instead of the one true God.

Meanwhile, Moses was having a happy time up the mountain talking to God. God wrote the Ten Commandments on two large pieces of stone, and Moses could hardly wait to get back to the people and show them.

On his way down the hill, Moses strained his eyes to get a glimpse of the Israeli camp. But wait! Something was going on. It looked like a feast or celebration. And what was that huge thing the people were dancing around? It looked like an idol. No, it could not be! Aaron, his own brother was in charge, and he would never let the people do such a wicked thing as that!

Moses was so upset that he threw the great stones on which God had written the Commandments down at his feet. They splintered into a million pieces. He said to Aaron, "How did the people get you to do such a terrible thing?"

Aaron was full of excuses for not doing what he should have done. "Oh, you know these people," he shrugged. "They're always getting into trouble. And I don't know how that calf got there. It just kind of popped out of the fire."

You can see that Aaron didn't think it was his fault at all . But God still held him responsible for all those people's sin. Because he was the one in charge.

BABY-SITTING

object lesson

physical activity

drama

Objective: to learn how to treat a baby.

Materials needed: a doll or stuffed animal.

Demonstrate the following actions on the "baby." Is it appropriate behavior? Your child should state "yes" or "no".

(1) Hold the baby's head up by placing a hand behind its neck.

(2) Let it play with pennies or small objects.

(3) Sing softly to it.

(4) Swing it by its hair.

(5) Change its diapers when wet.

(6) Let it chew on an electrical cord.

(7) Burp it over your shoulder after a feeding.

(8) Scream or clap loudly in its ear.

(9) Gently move its limbs.

(10) Lay it on the edge of a bed or chair.

Think of the heavy responsibility Moses and Aaron shouldered in leading the Children of Israel. Let your child practice responsibility by demonstrating proper baby care.

MIXED FEELINGS

our **world**   word **concepts**

Objective: to compare *happy* and *sad* emotions.

Talk about the feelings Moses must have experienced coming down the mountain. He was *happy* about the wonderful time he had spent with God. He was *sad* over the wickedness of the people while he was away. What does a person look like when he is happy? When he is sad? Ask your child how he would feel in the following situations.

(1) You can make it all the way across the monkey bars.

(2) You get a sore throat and stuffy nose.

(3) Mom or Dad is reading a favorite book to you.

(4) You leave a favorite sweater at a park.

(5) You go out with a grandparent for a treat.

(6) You tell your brother a lie.

(7) You share a toy with a friend.

(8) You accidentally spill your milk.

FIRST IMPRESSIONS

pre- **reading**   arts/ **crafts**

Objective: to identify letters of the alphabet.
Materials needed: light cardboard, scissors, paper, and crayons.

Cut out the following letters from cardboard: *A*, *M*, *G*, and *I*. These letters stand for the main characters in the Bible story: Aaron, Moses, God, and Israel. Put each one under a separate piece of paper. Peel the paper off a crayon and have your child rub it lengthwise across the paper to make an impression of the letters that are underneath. Help him to hold the paper and letter steady. What letter is it? Who does it stand for in the Bible story?

CAREFUL COOK

skill   object **lesson**   pre- **math**   physical **activity**

Objective: to see the importance of responsibility in the kitchen.
Materials needed: recipe and ingredients.

Pick out an easy recipe. Set the ingredients before your child. Carefully measure out the correct amounts and follow the recipe meticulously. After the food is prepared, take the same set of ingredients and let your child mix the amounts and prepare the recipe in any way he chooses. You have both used the same ingredients, but one recipe was prepared responsibly, the other was not. Compare results. Which one tastes better?

WEEK TWO

ANY FISH?

story

Objective: to encourage unquestioning obedience.

Tell the story of Simon Peter found in Luke 5. Relate a story from your own past when obedience didn't seem to make any sense at the time, but later you found out the reasons for its importance. Share a part of yourself.

Simon was tired and discouraged as he stood on the shore washing his smelly fish-nets and folding them flat for another day. He and his brother had fished all night and not caught a single thing.

When Jesus asked him to take the boat out into the deep water and let out the nets again, Simon tried to explain how he felt, but ended up saying that he would obey. That was one of the smartest things he ever decided to do — obey Jesus!

As soon as the nets struck the water, a mighty group of fish swarmed into them and became trapped. The load was far too much for one boat to manage, so Simon called out to his friends in another boat and they came to help. The nets broke under the heavy weight and now the two ships began to sink.

Simon was so surprised and amazed that he decided right on the spot to obey Jesus *whenever* He asked. So when Jesus suggested Simon follow Him and become a "fisher of men," Simon did just that.

SEE THE SEA

science · crafts · activity

Objective: to review the Bible story and discuss sea life.

Materials needed: sponges and scissors.

Cut some sea creatures out of the sponges. Make a fish, octopus, anemone, lobster, sea horse, or eel. Don't worry about authentic detailing; you'll have to keep it simple. Have some bathtub fun with the water toys you've made. Talk about how real sponges come from actual underwater animals. Discuss how they see, sleep, eat, and maneuver in their liquid environment. Which of these water animals filled Simon's nets?

HOLE AT THE BOTTOM OF THE SEA

concepts · science · activity

Objective: to define *deep* and *shallow*.

Materials needed: hand spade, jar, soil, and water.

Take some soil samples from your yard. Try to procure dirt from different strata. Dig *shallow* holes and take specimens. Add more dirt from several layers as you dig even *deeper*. Put the soil in a jar. Fill almost to the top with water, secure a lid and shake. Place the jar on a table and view the settlement process over time. Compare the colors and levels of soil by using the words deep and shallow prolifically. Did Jesus ask Peter to take his boat into deep or shallow water? Did he obey? Did he want to?

FUNNY FISH

reading · game · activity

Objective: to recognize and identify alphabetical letters.

Materials needed: a stick, string, paper clip, construction paper, and a pen.

Tie a string to the end of a stick to make a fishing pole. To the other end of the string, attach a paper clip. Let the child go fishing by casting his line over the sofa or an upended table where you can sit unseen. Fasten a construction paper fish to the paper clip. Give a little tug and let your child reel in his catch. Written on the fish should be an alphabetical letter. Let him state the name of the letter before casting out again.

FISHERS OF MEN

concepts · game · activity

Objective: to review the Bible story and concept words.

Materials needed: sieve and various items that can be submerged.

Fill a basin with water. Drop in the objects you have collected to represent fish. Some should sink and some should float. Let your child use the sieve as a net and "snag" as many fish as he can. Contrast shallow and deep as your child must go to different levels to scoop up the catch. See if he can keep all the "fish" in the "net" while he is still trying for more. Imagine how exhausted Simon must have felt after trying all night for just one fish. Was the Lord asking him to do something easy? Think about what it meant when Jesus later asked him to fish for men.

WEEK THREE

OBEYING THE RULES

story   crafts

Objective: to understand that God sees disobedience.

Materials needed: paper and crayons.

Tell the story of Achan's sin from Joshua 7. Relate the narrative event by event and have your child draw a picture to illustrate each scene.

What a marvelous victory at Jericho! All the people did was march around the walls and the whole city came crashing to the ground. Now they were ready for the next adventure. They were to take over the little town of Ai. But when their army came up to the walls, they were fiercely chased away and thirty-six men were killed. What went wrong?

Joshua prayed to God about it. God answered, saying that there was a man in the nation of Israel who had disobeyed. This person had stolen clothes and money. Because

one man had not obeyed the law, God let *all* of Israel lose the battle.

Joshua decided to find out who that one man was. He had all the people march in front of him until God showed him the right tribe, then the right family, then the right man. His name was Achan. Joshua asked him right out, "Son, what did you do?"

Achan hung his head and said, "I know God told us not to take anything from the city of Jericho. But I saw such a beautiful coat and some silver and a huge wedge of gold. I thought it would be a shame to leave them for someone else to find and steal, so I took them and hid them under the floor of my tent."

Achan and his whole family were punished severely. Joshua wanted him to know that you can't sin in secret. God sees every time we are disobedient. Just like Achan, we need to learn to obey.

HUNTING FOR LOOT

game   lesson   activity

Objective: to review the Bible story.

Materials needed: coins and a small garment.

Hide some money and clothing under a throw rug. Let your child know what he is looking for, then let him hunt around the house for the "stolen goods." When he finds them, discuss how Achan hid the same type of thing under the floor of his tent. He didn't want anybody to know he had disobeyed. Did anybody know?

JUMPING ROPE

game   lesson   activity

Objective: to point out the difference between *right* and *wrong*.

Materials needed: a rope.

Let your child practice jumping rope. Tie

one end to a post or a chair if you are the only rope-turner. Start by swinging the rope slowly back and forth under the child's legs if it is too hard for him to manage the jump when the rope is coming from overhead. Recite the following jumping rhyme in rhythm to the turning of the rope.

> Down by the ocean, down by the sea,
> Johnny broke a bottle and blamed it on me.
> I told ma, ma told pa.
> Johnny got a spankin' so ha, ha, ha.
> How many spankings did Johnny get? One, two, three....

After the game is over, talk about the poem. What did Johnny do *wrong*? Could he hide his sin? What happened to him for lying? Was the sister or brother *right* to be happy that Johnny got in trouble? Talk about how all of Israel suffered when Achan sinned.

TEN COMMANDMENTS

pre-reading   word concepts   paper-work

Objective: to see God's standards and practice writing numbers.
Materials needed: activity sheet (p. 125) and a pencil.

Talk about what God says is right and wrong. Write the correct numbers in the squares.

DOING WHAT'S RIGHT

music   word concepts   physical activity

Objective: to ingrain the principle of hearing and obeying.
Materials needed: the activity sheet (p. 127).

Teach the song to the tune of "Here We Go 'Round the Mulberry Bush." Make sure your child understands what the words mean. Sing and dance around in a circle as the instructions indicate.

INSTANT OBEDIENCE

story   object lesson   physical activity

Objective: to show how God wishes us to obey right away.
Materials needed: child's riding toy: a bike, trike, scooter, etc.

Have your child race you down the sidewalk. Give him two advantages: a vehicle and a head start. Have a wild chase and give him a run for his money. Use this as an introduction to the story of Philip (Acts 8) who was instructed by God to sprint and catch a chariot.

Imagine you were Philip and God told you one day to head south into the desert near Gaza. Well, I don't know about you, but Philip was used to obeying the Word of the Lord and he left immediately. Almost as soon as he arrived, he spotted a very fancy chariot traveling along the road at a pretty fast pace. A man was sitting in it. He was reading the Bible with a very confused look on his face.

God told Philip to catch up with him. Philip really had to jog to stay alongside the moving chariot, but he wouldn't disobey God for the world. So he ran as fast as he could and called out to the man, "Do you understand what you are reading?"

"How can I unless someone explains it to me?" the man replied. "Won't you please join me in the chariot so we can talk about it?" Philip hopped right up beside the man and had a perfect chance to tell him all about Jesus.

The man was so excited about Philip's words that as soon as they saw a little lake, he begged, "Is there any reason why I couldn't be baptized right here and now?"

Philip wanted to make sure the man truly believed that Jesus was God and Savior.

When Philip saw that he did, they wheeled the chariot off the road and parked by the side of the lake. After Philip had helped the man in and out of the water to show on the outside how he was being cleaned up on the inside, Philip disappeared! God whisked him away to do another job for Him. People who are willing to obey God, often lead very exciting lives!

WHICH WAY TO GO?

skill   arts/crafts

Objective: to work at making and following directions.
Materials needed: paper, colored markers, and a small prize: a sticker, cookie, barrette, etc.

Have your child work on a map to show another person how to get to a store, your church, or a friend's house. After it is completed, have him describe to you what he has written and what it means. (Do not expect any measure of perfection; this is just to get him thinking.) While he is working on this project, you can be drawing a very simplistic map of the room that you are in, with an X indicating where you have hidden a little prize. Help him to read and understand what you have drawn. Let him retrieve the prize for himself.

FOLLOWING DIRECTIONS

word concepts   game   physical activity

Objective: to continue the theme of listening and obeying.

Remind your youngster of the Bible story and how Philip followed directions as specifically and quickly as possible. Review which

is the left hand and which is the right. Give a series of commands that will lead your child to a specific place. For example, you might say, "Follow my instructions to find something that rhymes with *head.*" Then give a succession of orders, "Turn right, turn left, about-face…." Eventually lead him to a *bed.* Do it several times, always with a different goal in mind.

LEFT TO RIGHT

skill   pre-reading   word concepts   physical activity

Objective: to reinforce that we read from *left* to *right* and to teach a new task.

Show your child how to vacuum a room. He should not wheel the vacuum in a hodgepodge of different directions, but start at one side, pushing back and forth until he reaches the other wall. Start him on the *left* side, and let him work his way toward the *right.* Show him that you read a book the same way, left to right. Read one of his favorite stories together, using your finger to point to the words you are speaking.

REACHING THE LOST

skill   object lesson   our world

Objective: to give your child a burden for unbelieving people everywhere.
Materials needed: a magazine and scissors.

Have your child cut "people" pictures out of the magazine. Be sure to include people from every nationality and background. Hold the pictures up one at a time and ask, "Does this person need God? How about this one?" Talk about why people everywhere need God.

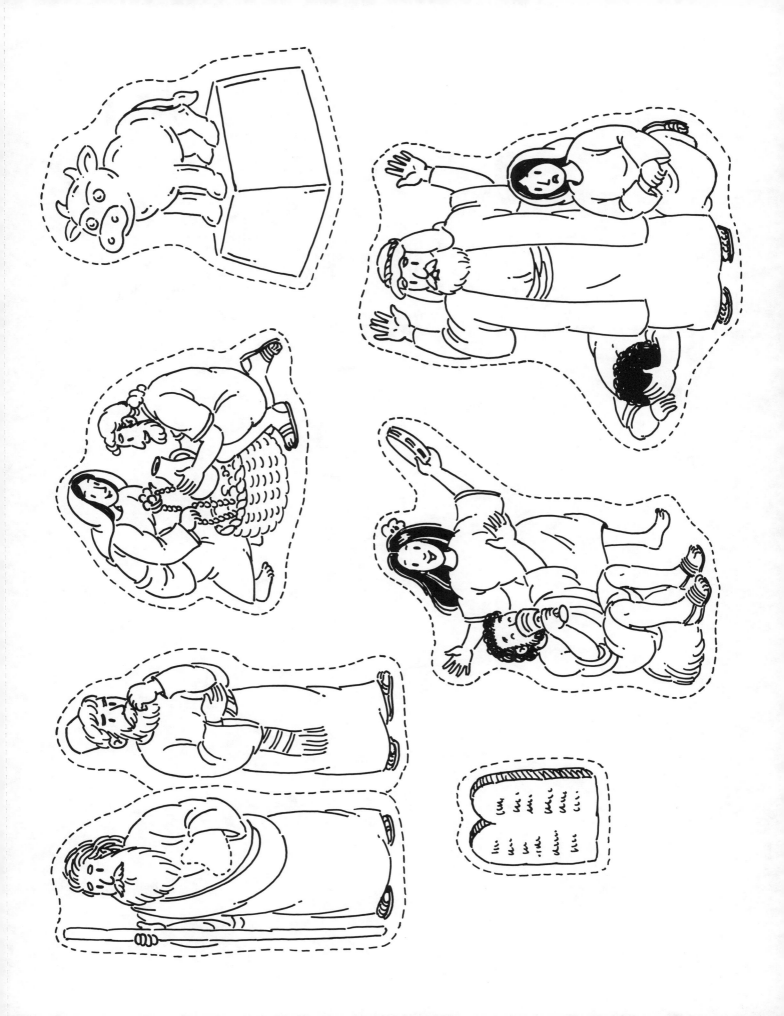

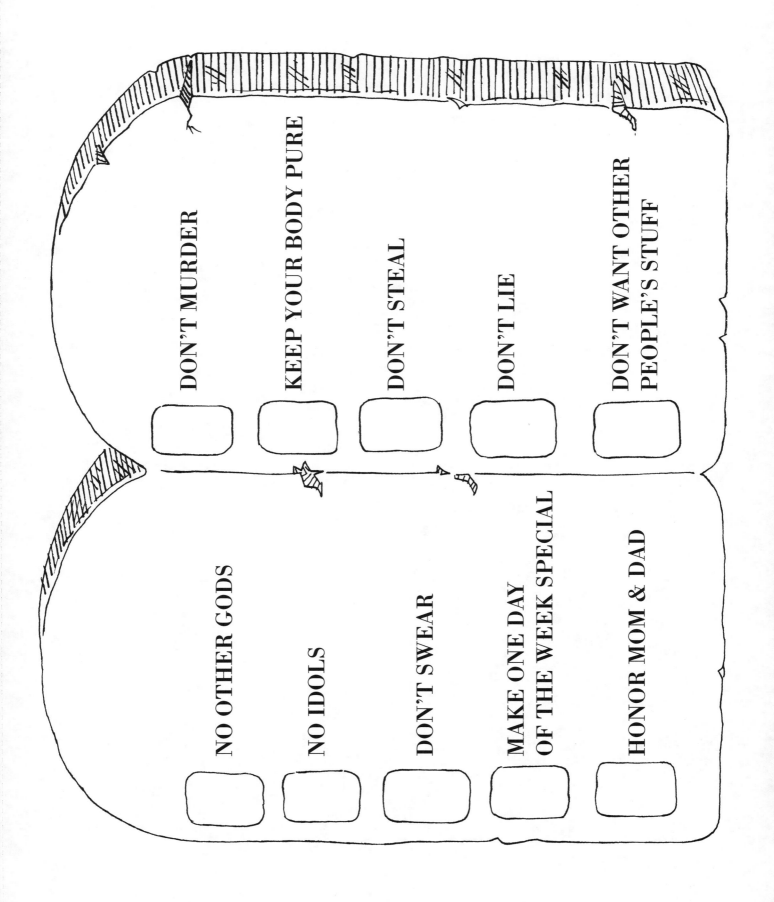

(1) hold hands and circle right   (2) circle left   (3) circle right   (4) circle left   (5) fall down

(1) I   know I ought to   do what's right   (2) to   love the Lord and

fol - low Him (3) to   hear just what He   says to me (4) o-

bey - ing all His   Word. (5)

AUGUST
WEEK ONE

LITTER BUG

Objective: to point out the responsibility God gave us when he placed us on the earth.

Do a little skit for your child. Pretend you are a careless, irresponsible camper who disregards the beauty of nature and destroys or trashes whatever he's around. Pretend to eat something and throw the wrapper on the ground. Be careless with imaginary matches. Waste water, pull up wildflowers, and chase forest animals. After you've made a royal mess of things, let your child point out everything you did wrong. Remind your child that when God finished creating the earth, it was perfect. What happened? Then tell your child the following story.

Hello, hello, hello! Let me introduce myself. What? You can't see me? Don't worry about that. I'm here whether you see me or not. I'm a teeny, tiny bug that likes to live wherever you see trash or junk piled around. My name? Litter Bug. But you can call me Litter. Oh, yeah. I have lots of homes. Parks, bathrooms, beaches, sidewalks...just about anywhere people are, you'll find me. People are always throwing candy wrappers, banana peels, old movie tickets, chewed up pieces of gum, empty potato chip bags, and all kinds of things on the ground. And don't I love it! I just love to crawl around on anything dirty and ugly.

Uh oh! What is that I see? Is that a boy and a girl coming toward me? They aren't picking up trash and throwing it away, are they? No, please, no! Don't let them do that. They are putting all the yucky, dirty things in the trash container. I'm doomed! Things will never be messy and horrid as long as there are children like that in the world. Don't they know that as long as things are neat and clean, my life as a filthy germ is over?

Help!

ECOLOGY

Objective: to excite your child about saving and reusing.
Materials needed: recyclable items and a large bag.

Explain to your child that to recycle is to take an item whose value is gone and make something else out of it that a person can use. Pull from a bag several items from around your house that could be recycled: a newspaper, glass soda bottle, a plastic liter container, an aluminum can, etc. Talk about what a recycling center would do with each one. What could the item be made into? Can your family do more in the area of recycling?

WINDOW WASHING

Objective: to see *dirty* become *clean*.
Materials needed: two pieces of old cloth and a window washing solution.

Find a window that needs washing. Put your child on one side and you on the other. Look through the *dirty* glass. Together, wipe away the grime and watch your faces become *cleaner* and brighter. Show your child how fun it is to keep his surroundings clean and cared for.

DUST DRAWINGS

pre-reading

word concepts

physical activity

Objective: to give another chance to practice letter writing.

Find a flat, dusty surface. (Look on top of a bookshelf or refrigerator. Use a ladder or stepstool if needed.) Write letters with your fingers in the light dirt. Finish by wiping the surface clean. As you wash away every spot of dirt, compare it to God washing the sin from our hearts. Is this God's way of recycling lives?

RECYCLING

our world

arts/crafts

Objective: to reuse an item ordinarily discarded, thus relieving a portion of the trash burden.
Materials needed: toilet paper tubes, paint, glitter, and brushes.

Decorate the tubes however desired. Let them dry. They can hold wound up extension cords when not in use. This keeps the cords from becoming tangled and entwined. Talk again about how God gave people a responsibility to care for the earth.

W E E K   T W O

LOT'S WIFE

story

object lesson

Objective: to show the consequences of disobedience.
Materials needed: salt.

Sprinkle the table with salt. Taste it. Draw in it. Put it in piles. Talk about the good

things it can do. Tell the child about one time when salt did not bring good or happiness. Start the story found in Genesis 19.

The angels had waited for Lot as long as they could. They kept warning him, "Get out of here as fast as you can. This is a wicked place. If you do not leave immediately, you will be destroyed!" But he diddled and dawdled until finally the angels grabbed his arm, the arm of his wife, and the arms of his daughters and pulled them out of the city.

"Run!" they screamed. "Run for your lives. Do not look back but keep going until you reach the mountain." The angels knew that fire and scalding rocks would be pouring down from the sky and the only way Lot and his family could escape would be to follow their advice.

Lot and his daughters listened and obeyed. But Lot's wife hesitated. Perhaps she was thinking about all the nice things she had left behind, or perhaps she really did not believe that anything terrible was about to happen. At any rate, she disobeyed and turned around for one last look. In that very instant, she turned into a block of salt—a solid pillar of hard, white salt!

What a terrible thing it is to disobey.

DANGER SIGN

arts/crafts

our world

word concepts

physical activity

Objective: to review and stress parental warnings for safety.
Materials needed: a piece of cardboard, paint, and a brush.

Work together on making a sign that reads DANGER. Look around the house and yard for places to hang the sign. Are there any spots that require this extra warning? Around what should a young child be careful? What warning should Lot's wife have heeded?

SAFETY CHECK

concepts   work   world

Objective: to be able to spot potential hazards and to contrast the words *safe* and *dangerous*.

Materials needed: crayons and the activity sheet (p. 135).

Talk about how Lot should have thought ahead and seen the danger into which he was leading his family. How could they have avoided trouble in the first place? Look at the page to see some catastrophes about to happen. Circle potential places of *danger*. How could they be avoided and the area made *safe?*

CRISIS CALLS

math   skill   world

Objective: to prepare the child for emergency situations and to review numbers that are vital to his wellbeing.

Do some telephone practice. Review emergency numbers. How and when do you use them? What should your child say when he calls? Rehearse your own number. Let your child dial or punch the numbers into the phone.

'CHUTES AND 'COPTERS

game   world

Objective: to see the rewards of obedience and the consequences of disobedience.

Materials needed: tokens, a die, and the activity sheet (p. 137).

Play the game by progressing from number one through number 42. Throw the die and move the numbers indicated. The first person to reach the pilot's medal wins. If you land on a square with a helicopter, you advance to a reward. If you land on a parachute, you descend to a consequence.

WEEK THREE

LAUGHING HYENA

story   game

Objective: to see the importance of obedience in the area of decorum.

Tell the following story about the disobedient little hyena. After the story, have your child recite a poem or verse to you. Every time he begins, start chatting about the weather or discussing the price of tomatoes. Can he talk to you and listen at the same time? Show how important it is to be quiet and respectful whenever we have an opportunity to hear about God.

The little hyena stood very still to allow his mother to button the last button of his stiff white shirt. "Now Henry," his mother pleaded softly, "please sit still and behave in church. But most of all—do not start to giggle." Mama shook her head as she remembered last Sunday. Henry had done fine until old Mrs. Trumble had gotten up to sing a solo. As soon as her squeaky voice crackled on a high note, Henry started squirming with laughter. Hiding his face in his sleeve, he snorted and chuckled until he was rolling in the pew. Mama had to take him out to let him get hold of himself. If there was anything Henry liked to do, it was laugh. Mama sighed. He would have to learn that there are some times and places when he needed to hold in the laughter. Henry needed to be more responsible.

Mama was proud as she glanced over at her little hyena during the service. He sang each song with gusto and when it was time for prayer, he folded his paws and closed his eyes. He enjoyed the choir number so much, he tapped his little toes in time to the music. But something went wrong when it was time to take the offering. Mama could tell by the twinkle in his eyes and the twitch of his lips that something had tickled Henry very much. She followed his gaze to the top of the usher's head. Yes, something was strange about the way Gerry the giraffe parted his hair today. Did he wear a wig? Because today it looked like it was on backward. Oh, dear.

By now Henry was snuffling with his paw over his mouth, ready to explode in a loud guffaw. Mama grabbed him by the ear and marched him out. "Henry!" she scolded firmly now that she had really gotten his attention. "You are responsible not only for the way you behave, but also for all the *others* that you bother as well. Now then. I have an assignment for you. There were three rows of animals sitting behind us. I want you to write a note to every single one this week. You need to tell them you are sorry for keeping them from hearing God's voice this morning. You must be responsible!"

It was a more sober and smarter hyena that walked back into church behind his mama for the rest of the meeting. For the first time, he realized how many others were affected by the little things that he did.

TEA TIME

skill   activity

Objective: to provide a setting for propriety and manners.

Dress up for a special high afternoon or mid-morning tea. Serve a delectable drink in fancy cups with the best silver. Light some candles. Use cloth napkins.

As you are partaking, instruct your child and let him practice the finest in manners. Talk about why we should act in a polite and courteous way toward other people. When we are only in the presence of our family, do

we still need to be considerate?

QUIET AS A MOUSE

arts/crafts   word concepts   physical activity   music

Objective: to contrast the concept words *quiet* and *loud*.

Materials needed: small, empty raisin boxes, beans, rice, marbles, and sugar.

Talk about our behavior in church, libraries, stores, etc. Should we be *quiet* or *loud*? Make musical shakers by partially filling the raisin boxes with different substances. See if you can get an interesting rhythm going. Experiment to see which box is quiet and which is loud when shaken.

HYMN # 12

pre-math   our world   music

Objective: to find page numbers.

Materials needed: hymnbook or Bible and a rubber band.

Wrap a rubber band around all but the first twenty pages of your book. Let your child practice turning to a hymn or Scripture verse. Call out a page number and let him find the corresponding page. (Show him where the number can be found on the page and keep the numbers within the first twenty pages.) Describe how the ability to find page numbers can assist him in a worship service.

GOD'S MUSIC

our world   music   nature science

Objective: to show the benefits of quiet and to give an appreciation for the sounds that God created.

Find a park, forest, or backyard where you can lie on a blanket on the grass and listen to the sounds of nature. Be perfectly quiet until you can distinguish one sound from another. After each one becomes distinct in your ears, see if you can imitate the individual sounds you hear. Mimic the music of nature.

WEEK FOUR

RECHABITE FAMILY

story

Objective: to show that God honors obedience, especially when it is difficult.

Materials needed: a ribbon topped with a paper circle reading "#1."

Tell the following story of the family that refused to disobey, from Jeremiah 35. Think of a time when your child obeyed despite difficulties. Praise him for his actions and reinforce any determination to please you by presenting him with a homemade medal of valor.

The Rechabite family came into the room where Jeremiah the prophet already waited. They sat down around a table. Jeremiah asked that a jug of wine and a cup be set in front of each person. Then he told them, "Drink the wine."

The Rechabite family did not know what to do. They looked at the prophet and then at each other. But not one person reached out a hand to drink the wine. Almost as if they were one person, they said firmly, "No, we will not drink."

They made a decision to obey their father who had instructed them and their children never to drink wine. Jeremiah was pleased even though they did not do what he asked them to do. "I'm glad you decided to obey your father," he said. "I wish the rest of Israel would obey God as well as you obey your dad."

Later, when the Chaldeans came to capture the land, they wiped out all the people that lived in Israel and took them captive, except for one family—the Rechabites. God was pleased that they had learned to obey, and He protected them.

HAPPY ENDING

concepts

game

Objective: to note and determine *beginnings* and *endings*.

Ask your child to tell you the *beginning* and the *ending* of the Bible story about the Rechabites. Hunt up five or six of your child's favorite stories. Keep the book hidden, but read the beginning few lines and the concluding paragraph. With that much of a clue, let your child guess the name of the story. Mix up the beginning and end. Let him state which is which.

BAD HABITS

drama

activity

Objective: to look at addictions and habits with the purpose of avoiding and discarding them.

Talk about the wisdom of the Rechabites in refusing to drink strong wine. (One out of eight people that taste liquor of any kind become alcoholics.) What are some other habits to avoid? Discuss any problems your child might be working through: thumb sucking, fingernail chewing, bed wetting, temper tantrums, etc. Let your child start working with a stuffed animal toward a solution as if the animal had the same problem your child has. Will he give it extra love? Will he reward it for good behavior? Will he think of ways to give it reminders? Match your efforts with his and see if progress can be made.

CHRONOLOGICAL CUPS

pre-math

word concepts

object lesson

Objective: to review the Bible story and put the numbers in order from beginning to end.

Materials needed: ten cups, small squares of paper, tape, and a pen.

Stick the pieces of paper onto the cups. Let your child indicate with slashes or dots a different number on each one. Mix them up and place them all around the edge of a table. Remember the family that came into the room with Jeremiah and sat around a table with cups of wine? What did they say when the prophet asked them to disobey their father? Now ask your child to count the dots on the cups and place them in chronological order from smallest number to biggest. Bring in the concept words by having him show you the beginning and end of the line.

ORDERING EVENTS

word concepts

paper-work

Objective: to see in another form the concepts of beginning and end.

Materials needed: crayons and the activity sheet (p. 139).

Look at the pictures on the top row. Some show the beginning of an event and some show the end. Have your child match each picture on the top with a picture on the bottom. Then let him state which came first.

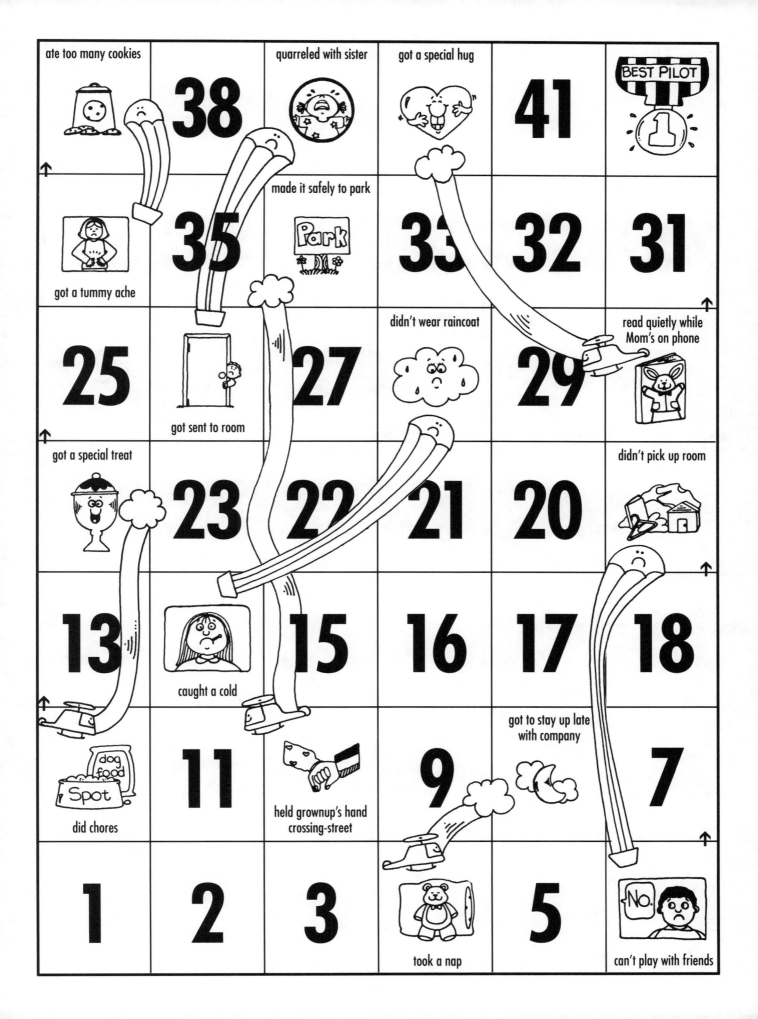

THEME: joy and thankfulness

INTRODUCTION

Dewey had the ball game tuned in on the radio. A fly buzzed on the windowpane. From down the street we could hear the music of an ice cream truck. The sofa felt hot and scratchy against our bare arms. The smell of honeysuckle wafted through the open window. Then the phone began to ring, and my son rushed into the room to pick up the receiver.

My four-year-old daughter Ashley and I were sitting together, trying to read a Bible story. But the first thing I needed to do

before I could accomplish anything was to convince her that of all the fascinating things that were going on in the world (every single one vying for her undivided attention at that precise moment), there was nothing more important than the principle she was about to learn from the story I would tell.

We were reading about a servant girl named Hagar and a time when her mistress Sarai was being nasty and mean. In desperation, Hagar ran away. She didn't know where to go or what to do. Just when she was at the point of giving up, God supplied an answer for her critical need. In amazement at his provision, she exclaimed, "You are the God who sees me!" That was the conviction I wanted Ashley to embrace—that we have a God who cares and watches over all that we do.

Deciding that bribes, threats, and theatrics would only temporarily capture interest, I opted to underscore the thrust of the story in terms of childhood impact. I wanted to create a hunger and a yearning for the very information I wished to impart. I turned to Ashley and asked, "Have you ever been afraid of anything? I mean really scared? So scared you thought you'd die?"

I already knew what the answer would be. Ashley's the one member of our family for whom a suggestion can induce a shiver. Merely the mention of lions and tigers and bears would send her clutching at my knees. But it was important for Ashley to be the one to interact with the question. She needed to come to the answer by herself. Her eyes grew wide at my query, and she gave a hearty nod. Quickly, I followed up on the thought. "Well, Hagar was also afraid," I told Ashley. "She was all alone and didn't know what to do." I could tell by her sudden attentiveness that I'd gotten Ashley hooked. But now it was up to me to carry the whole concept from beginning to end without dropping the ball.

Imparting truth requires much more than simply passing out the information. Ashley needed to be able to do more than rehearse back to me the fact that "God watches over us and sees everything we do." Grasping the general idea is never enough. She needed to reevaluate what she already thought she knew—to weigh existing knowledge against brand-new truth. I wanted her to be stirred emotionally, to be deeply moved within her soul. Then, I also knew that the concept must pique her curiosity enough to cause her to ask questions and desire to hear more. Finally, to really accomplish the maximum result, I should be able to observe a change in her lifestyle or behavior. I had to lead my

daughter through every single one of these steps in order for learning to take place in the heart as well as the head.

As Ashley and I read through the story together, I made sure that she could understand the meaning of all the words and phrases that were being used. No reason for a language barrier to block her comprehension from the very beginning. I didn't feel an obligation, however, to recite every last detail of the story. Preschooler's attention spans are very short and parts of the narrative would have been hard for her to understand. On the other hand, I did not want to reinterpret Scripture in my efforts to make things simple; I just stuck with the main theme. At the conclusion of the story, I asked her questions to encourage verbalization. I wanted to clarify that everything had been communicated and understood. Ashley seemed proud to be able to tell parts of the story back to me. We even acted it out, Ashley playing the part of Hagar and I the angry mistress.

Now came the most important part: personal application. "If you were deep-sea diving at the bottom of the ocean, could God see you there? If you flew in a rocket to the moon? If you stole a cookie from the cookie jar? If you screamed at your brother? If you were in a dark place and very afraid? How about if you got lost from your mom and dad in a department store? Would God know where you were?" As I asked each question, I could see by Ashley's expressions that she was troubled to think that God could see her wrongdoing and relieved to know that He would care for her in trouble. Good. Those were the very responses I was hoping for.

A bit later, it was time to bring it even closer to home. I wanted to apply the lesson to Ashley's own personal fear. She had been recently petrified over the thought of meeting strange dogs. If we were on a walk, and someone passed by with a dog (even on a leash), Ashley would scream and practically shinny up my legs in an effort to make it to higher and safer ground. I opened our discussion by reminding her of some recent incidents in which this fear had obsessed her actions. My intention was not to reprimand, but to include these experiences under the category of "times when God watches over Ashley." But we needed a visual reminder for the next time a similarly stressful situation would occur. So we went to the table and worked together on a colorful paper bracelet inscribed with the words, "You are the God who sees me." Since Ashley could not yet read, we drew eyes all around the letters to remind her of the watchful eyes of God.

Now in the evening, when it was time for us to take our stroll around the block, she would have an ever-present reminder that she did not have to fear the bites of a big dog, but she could trust in the same God that provided for Hagar. Few behavioral traits, particularly fears, disappear immediately. (Think of your own tendencies to worry.) I was aware of that. I knew that the first time Ashley saw a dog again, I'd be prying her fingers off my legs. But alongside that fear would be a new awareness. And when she made it by the animal unscathed, it would be added affirmation that God had once more been faithful and provided escape.

Over the days and weeks to come, as I reviewed and reminded, Ashley became stronger and more established in her trust. We added other stories and made up some simple songs to reinforce her newfound con-

viction. Then one day she even reached out a hand to a friendly puppy and delighted in its affectionate slobberings.

I finally realized that the lesson had been fully assimilated when I overheard Ashley telling a friend about how she "used to be scared of dogs. But I'm not anymore." That was the best conclusion I could ever hope for. The picture was complete. Now she was seeking to reproduce her change in the life of another by sharing what had happened in her own words.

The Lord uses the same teaching methods with us. When He wants us to understand His love, for example, He catches our attention by revealing our need for Him. He is not satisfied with a liturgical grasp of any concept; He wishes us to accept it with our mind, will, and emotions. He explains and demonstrates His love in a myriad of different words and forms, hoping that somehow one will swing wide the door of comprehension and the light of the truth will flood through. He then requires personal application and acceptance. He is patient when we forget what we know to be true. He gives us constant reminders until there has been total assimilation. He looks for a change in behavior and lifestyle and is delighted to see His children passing on to others what they have learned. He is the perfect father and the perfect teacher.

SEPTEMBER
WEEK ONE

TEN LEPERS

story

drama

Objective: to show two possible responses to blessing—thankfulness and ingratitude.

Ask how your child would feel if no one wanted to be around him any more. What if people always looked the other way when they saw him? What if they walked to the other side of the street when he passed by? What if no one wanted to eat with him, hug him, play with him, or tuck him in bed? How would he feel? Use this as an introduction to the following story (found in Luke 17:11-19) of the lepers who surely would have felt like outcasts among friends and family.

"Master, look at us! Feel sorry and help us!" Ten men were standing far away and calling for Jesus. As soon as He saw them, Jesus knew they were lepers. A leper is a person who has a disease that eats away his skin. Lepers had to stand far back from other people because no one else wanted to catch the disease. A leper could not even go back to his family after being healed without being examined by the priest to make sure the leprosy was totally gone.

Jesus did feel sorry for the poor, outcast men. He told them, "Go, and show yourselves to a priest." As the men turned away to do what Jesus said, they looked down at their skin. Wow! The leprosy was all gone! The sores on their skin were completely healed. They could not wait to be checked by a priest so they could get back to their families and friends. So they hurried as fast as they could down the road.

But one of them remembered the goodness of the Lord in deciding to heal him at all. He was so thankful that he just had to tell Jesus right away. Running back to where Jesus stood, he threw himself down on the ground and praised God in a loud voice.

Jesus looked around. "Didn't I heal *ten* men who had leprosy? I only see *one* that is giving glory to God. Where are the other nine?" Where would you be?

TWO PERSPECTIVES

object lesson

our world

Objective: to see that we don't wait for perfect conditions to be thankful.
Materials needed: two grapes and a raisin.

Set up an imaginary play, starring two grapes as the main characters. Begin by explaining that in order for grapes to grow up into juicy and delicious fruit, they need just the right amount of rain to make them plump and just the right amount of sun to make them rosy. Grape #1 lives in Oregon. The weather has been just perfect, one lovely day follows another. Grape #1 thanks the Lord from the bottom of his heart for the care and kindness that has been shown in allowing him to become healthy and happy. Grape #2 lives in California. There is a drought in his valley, and the vines have not received as much water as they had in other years. Is grape #2 angry at God when the hot sun burns down on his skin and makes it shrivel and turn brown? Oh, no! Because grape #2 knows that even though everything has not been perfect and it seems sometimes that God does not care, God still has a perfect plan in mind. In fact, He has brought along the perfect conditions to make grape #2 a tasty and delectable RAISIN!

MOVING MEN

word concepts — paper-work

Objective: to contrast the words *moving* and *still.*

Materials needed: crayons, scissors, and the activity sheet (p. 153).

Review the Bible story while making a visual aid that allows the ungrateful men to *move* away from the Lord while the thankful one remains *still* at the feet of Jesus.

CHECKLIST

pre-math — physical activity

Objective: to give opportunity for counting and thinking about the elimination of injury and disease.

Materials needed: first-aid kit.

Either put together a small first-aid kit or use an already existing one in your household. Make a checklist of everything that is in the box. Read off the items and how many of each there ought to be. Let your child count the corresponding items. If the numbers are the same, he can place a small X by the item on the list, signifying you have all you need. Talk about how such a kit can help with injury and disease.

COUNT YOUR BLESSINGS

arts/crafts

Objective: to give a visual reminder of all the things for which we can be thankful.

Materials needed: drinking straws, marking pen, and paper baking cups.

Chat together about what kinds of things ought to make us grateful. Write each idea in the middle of a baking cup. Twist each cup in the center, leaving the outer edges splayed out so that it resembles a flower. Stick each bloom into the end of a drinking straw to give it a stem. After you have made a number of blossoms, arrange them in a vase as a centerpiece. After dinner, let each family member open a flower or two and thank God for the blessing that is written on the inside.

WEEK TWO

SINGING HIS PRAISE

story — music

Objective: to see that thankfulness has no relationship to circumstance.

Read the following story taken from 2 Chronicles 20. After you have told it in your own words, decide on a cheerful song for your child to sing whenever he gets low or is facing a scary situation that he can't handle alone.

King Jehoshaphat was in big trouble. He didn't know what to do. A huge enemy army was coming, and there was no way his little band of Israeli soldiers could fight and win. So the king cried out to God, "What shall I do?"

God answered and said, "Don't be afraid. This battle is not yours but mine. You won't even need to fight. Just stand and watch. I'll take care of everything."

So the next day Jehoshaphat chose from among the people the very best musicians in all the land. These people went in front of the army and began to sing and praise God. Here they were, going out to battle, lifting up their voices with beautiful songs for God. Can you imagine what the enemy army must have thought?

But it doesn't much matter what they thought because right away God confused the enemy so much that they started to kill each other. By the time the dust had settled, not one evil soldier was left. The good Israeli soldiers had not even taken the swords out of their belts.

God was pleased that King Jehoshaphat had been joyful and thankful even in trouble. The enemy soldiers left many riches in the field where they died, and God allowed the Israelites to keep the precious jewels and treasures that they found.

SPOON TUNE

music   science   physical activity

Objective: to learn a new way to make music.
Materials needed: seven glasses filled with water to different heights and a spoon.

Make a note by tapping the glasses of water with a spoon. Together, put them in order, lowest to highest. Play some tunes and enjoy the music. Remember the children of Israel who made music and praised God in spite of their fears.

NAME THAT TUNE

word concepts   music

Objective: to learn to *stop* and *go* within the theme of music.

Pick some familiar music tapes to insert in a tape player. Pop them in one at a time and start the music when your child says, *"Go"* Play the tape until he can identify and recognize the tune. Let him shout, *"Stop,"* as soon as he knows the song. (A variation on this game would be to hum a tune until the child recognizes it and shouts, "Stop.")

STOP LIGHT

pre-reading   word concepts   arts/crafts   game   physical activity

Objective: to give more stop and go practice and a chance to write.
Materials needed: paper, markers, cup, and a toy car.

Make three circles, one on the top of the other. Red should be at the top, yellow in the middle and green at the bottom. Help your child to write the words *stop*, *slow*, and *go* in their respective circles. Let him drive a car around the floor following the appropriate instruction, based upon the color circle to which you are pointing.

After the game, think about God's encouragement to King Jehoshaphat to "stand still and watch the salvation of the Lord." To obey, would the Children of Israel have to stop or go?

THANK YOU, JESUS

music   skill   physical activity

Objective: to learn a happy ditty that brings glory to God.
Materials needed: activity sheet (p. 155).

Rehearse a thankfulness song based on the tune "Skip to My Lou." Sing a number of verses inserting slaps, whistles, snaps, clucks, sniffs, and stomps in place of claps.

WEEK THREE

JOYFUL JOB

story   drama

Objective: to see that gratitude is an attitude.
Materials needed: six small pebbles or sticks.

As you tell the following story, taken from the Book of Job, place two pebbles on the table to represent Job and his wife. Each time a messenger comes in with a new piece of devastating news, trot in another pebble and place it next to Job. When his wife advises him to "curse God and die," take away all the pebbles, and leave Job all by himself.

There once was a man who was richer than any other man in the whole country. His name was Job. He was a good man and pleased God.

But one day a messenger came to him and said, "Your cows and donkeys were working and feeding when a band of wild men fell on them and stole every one. They killed all the servants, but I alone escaped to tell you."

While he was still speaking, another messenger came. "Fire fell from heaven," this one reported, "and burned up all your sheep and shepherds. I alone escaped to tell you."

While he was still speaking, another messenger came. "An enemy surrounded your camels and took them away," he cried. "They killed all your servants that were watching them, but I alone escaped to tell you."

While he was speaking, another messenger came. "Your sons and daughters were having a party at the oldest brother's house," he breathlessly explained. "A great wind hit the outside walls, and they collapsed on top of your family. They are all dead, but I alone escaped to tell you."

Job stood up and in spite of all the things that he had just heard, said calmly, "The Lord gives things to us, and the Lord takes things away from us. Praise the name of the Lord."

A little bit later, Job's skin broke out with some very painful sores. Nothing he could do would make them stop hurting. His wife said, "Tell God how awful He is for doing these terrible things to you!" When he refused to say anything bad about God, she left him.

Soon others came to stare at him and laugh at his misery. Could anything be worse? All he could do was lie in a pit and scrape at his wounds with bits of pottery and moan. Still, as he sat in ashes, he thanked and praised God for being so wonderful.

God was pleased. Job was rich at the beginning of the story, but God made him twice as wealthy at the end. God gave him more sheep, camels, donkeys, and cows than ever before. He received a whole new family, and his friends and relatives came back and gave him many gifts. Job lived a long life and was abundantly blessed by God.

TASTE TEST

Objective: to be in the place of a sufferer and to realize the importance of our senses.
Materials needed: an apple and a potato.

Cut the inside of an apple and a potato into identical slices. By appearance, can you tell them apart? Have your child hold his nose and take a bite. Can he identify them now? When he is allowed to use his sense of smell, are the tastes more distinct? Imagine what he would hear, feel, smell, see, and taste if he were sick like Job and every comfort was gone.

FIVE SENSES

Objective: to make a food item that uses every one of your child's senses while illustrating soft and hard.
Materials needed: popcorn and a popper or a skillet with oil, or microwave popcorn and a microwave.

Make popcorn together. Talk about the sound, sight, smell, feel, and taste. Note the difference between the soft and puffy result and the original hard kernels.

YARN LETTERS

pre-reading   word concepts   arts/crafts   physical activity

Objective: to feel the difference between *hard* and *soft* and to form alphabetical letters.

Materials needed: glue, yarn, and a small, hard surface like tile, wood, or shingle to be used as a background.

Dip small lengths of yarn into glue and form them into letters on the background you have selected. Contrast the feeling of the two substances. Which one is *soft* and which one is *hard?* Talk about which one you would pick for a bed: a mattress stuffed with yarn, or a sheet covering a slab of tile? Think how miserable Job must have been to scrape at his sores with bits of broken pottery. Were they soft or hard? Even so, he was thankful to God.

HEAD BONGS

one world   nature science   physical activity

Objective: to give an auditory stimulation.

Materials needed: three feet of yarn and a wire hanger.

Tie both ends of a piece of yarn onto the straight bottom of a wire hanger. Slide the knots as far apart as possible. Drape the yarn over your head with the hanger suspended hook down under your chin. Make sure the yarn comes down over your ears. Cup your hands lightly on the yarn over your ears. Hang your head down until the hanger can swing freely back and forth. Crash it into the wall or a counter. Listen to the resonant bongs. Imagine you are listening to the chime of a great clock. Thank God for the ability to hear.

A FRIGHTENING DREAM

story   object lesson

Objective: to encourage your child to realize all that the Lord has given him.

After you read the following character story, take a peek together into your child's closet and toy box. Look at bookshelves and dresser drawers. Does he have a lot to be thankful for?

Diana rubbed her eyes and stared. She was in her bedroom all right but nothing was the same. Her bed was gone. She was lying on the cold, hard floor. Her bookcase, with all her lovely storybooks, was gone. The beautiful pink toy box was no longer against the wall, and there was not a toy to be seen. From where she was sitting, it looked like the closet was bare and all her clothes had disappeared. What was going on?

"Mom!" she called stepping out into the hall. Room by room she could see nothing but emptiness, and she didn't see any people around either. No brothers and sisters, not even a cat or a dog. She wanted to call her friend next door, but there was no telephone. Glancing out the door, she looked down the block for the familiar sight of the crossing guard at the corner. No one was there. Looking down the block the other way, she strained to see the owner of the little grocery store. Often at this time of morning he would be sweeping the sidewalk in front of the store. But the place looked deserted. Not even a car drove by.

This was too much for Diana. She sat down on the porch step and burst into tears. All she could remember were all the times she had complained about not having enough toys or enough clothes. Oh, if only she could have back the ones that were already hers, she knew she would never fuss again. And her family. What about all the times she had whined about having to share something with a brother or sister? Or wished that she were an only child so she would get more attention? Now she'd give anything to hear the footstep or feel the hand of one of the other kids on her shoulder. She missed them like crazy.

How about when she'd fussed about being too old to cross the street with the crossing guard? Or complained when Mom sent her down the block to pick up something at the little store? She longed to see a familiar face. And Mom and Dad. Where were they? Had she ever gotten upset at having to obey them? Well, not any more. She wished more than anything just to have a mom or dad at all. "Mommy, Daddy, where are you?" she cried out in desperation.

Suddenly, she felt a soft hand shaking her arm and heard a gentle voice calling her name. "Diana, wake up. Diana, are you having a bad dream? Diana…." She sat up with a start and gasped for joy. Her mother was right beside the bed, her room was all together, she could hear her brothers and sisters in other parts of the house, and she knew without looking that the crossing guard and grocer were doing their jobs down the street. Her friend would be playing quietly next door. It had all been a dream. Everything was back to normal. That is, everything but her heart. She was sure she would never be ungrateful again!

CAREGIVERS

game

physical
activity

Objective: to help your child be thankful for the help of all the grownups in his life: parents, grandparents, babysitters, church teachers, community helpers, etc.

Read the following list, one at a time. If the function is a job your child can handle alone,

let him stand up. If the task is too hard and should not be attempted without a grownup, have him sit down. Could your child get along without extra help? Talk about why your child made the choices he did.

(1) ironing clothes
(2) sorting clothes
(3) driving a car
(4) buckling a seat belt
(5) cooking on the stove
(6) stirring cookie dough
(7) plugging in a lamp cord
(8) turning on a lamp
(9) starting a fire in the fireplace
(10) picking up sticks for the fire

WRESTLING

game

word
concepts

physical
activity

Objective: to make a distinction between *strong* and *weak*.

Do some arm and thumb wrestling together. To arm wrestle, you must be seated facing one another with your right elbows resting on the table. Grasp hands. At a given signal, both wrestlers must push to the right, attempting to drive the competitor's arm into the table. To thumb wrestle, link the fingers of your right hands, thumbs in the air. At a given signal, both wrestlers must try to trap the competitor's thumb under his own. Give your child a run for his money, but don't completely wipe him out every time. Your goal is not to prove your own strength, but to contrast *strong* and *weak*. Are there any other ways a person can be strong, outside of the physical realm? See if your child can think of one person he admires in each of the following categories:

(1) strong prayer warrior
(2) strong encourager
(3) strong reader
(4) strong business person
(5) strong believer

VITAL STATS

  math **concepts**   **activity**

Objective: to carry on the comparison of strong and weak (giving your child reason to appreciate you as helper and nurturer) while learning about figures and numbers.

Materials needed: paper and pencil.

Make a chart for comparison of vital statistics. One column will represent you and the other your child. Let your child fill in all the numbers he can. How many steps does it take for you to cross the room toe to toe? How far in inches can you fit your arm under a cabinet or dresser before the size of your arm restricts you? How many books can you stack and jump over before you knock the pile down? Think of your own contests for comparison.

BOOKMARK

arts/crafts **word** **concepts** **pre-** **reading**

Objective: to make a gift of appreciation for a caregiver while remembering our own source of strength.

Materials needed: scissors, construction paper, and markers.

Draw the simple outline of a bookmark-sized barbell (a rod with a weight at each end) on a piece of construction paper. Lightly outline the words to 2 Cor. 12:10, "When I am weak, then I am strong." Let your child cut out the symbol of strength and trace the words of the verse. Even when we do not feel mighty, God will give us the strength we need.

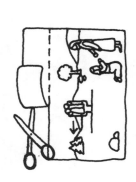

1. Cut out nine lepers.
2. Cut page and road on dotted lines.
3. Insert nine lepers in slit and move them down the road away from Jesus.

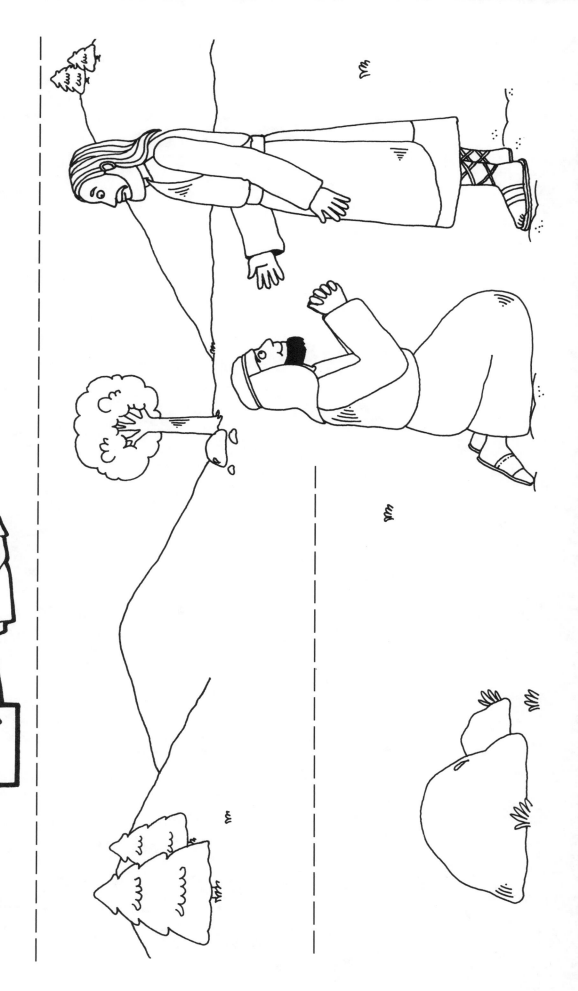

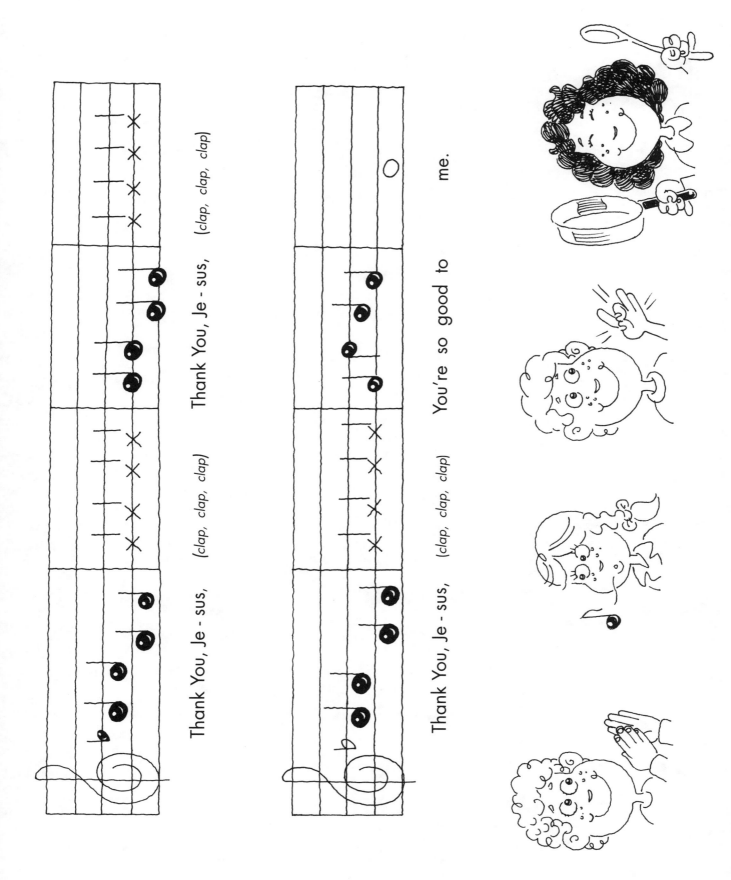

Thank You, Je - sus, (clap, clap, clap)   Thank You, Je - sus, (clap, clap, clap)

Thank You, Je - sus, (clap, clap, clap)   You're so good to   me.

OCTOBER
WEEK ONE

GOD'S BACK

story

game

Objective: to discuss the happiness that knowing God brings.
Materials needed: various household items.

Put your hand over your child's eyes. Lift your hand and let him briefly view the back of an object before you hide it completely away. Can he identify what it was from such a brief glance and unusual perspective? Use this as an introduction to the Bible story taken from Genesis 3 and Exodus 33.

The first man and woman lived in a beautiful garden called Eden. There were lots of things for them to enjoy and do during the day—swimming, playing, eating, and taking care of all the animals. But the one thing they looked forward to more than any other was their walk in the evening with God. Just as the sun was sinking behind the trees, they would stroll along together and talk and laugh and watch the stars come out. It made them all very happy.

But after Adam and Eve disobeyed God and chose to do wrong things, they could never again enjoy that wonderful walk. Things were different now. They could not see God face to face—neither could any of their children because they also chose to sin.

Many years later, Moses begged God, "Please, let me see You!" But God said, "I cannot let you see My face because I am so holy. It would hurt your eyes and you would die. But watch very carefully. I will let you stand in the mouth of a cave. I will pass by very quickly and put My hand on your eyes. Just at the last, I will take away My hand and you can see My back." Moses was glad even to see a little part of the Lord.

Just like Adam and Eve and Moses, it would hurt us to look right into God's face today. But we can still get to know Him even though we cannot see Him. Spending time with God is one of the happiest things we can do.

HOT AIR

object lesson

nature science

our world

physical activity

Objective: to visualize realities that cannot be seen in the physical and spiritual world.
Materials needed: two squares of tissue.

Have a contest with the tissue. Give a square to each person and see who can keep it in the air the longest by blowing from underneath. After several rematches to determine who has the most "hot air," consider the power that kept the tissue in the air. Could it be seen? But could you see what it did? Discuss other things that are invisible but nonetheless a reality: electricity, radio waves, smells, etc. What about God? Can He be real without being seen?

BACKWARD ALPHABET

pre-reading

word concepts

Objective: to contrast *forward* and *backward*, and to alleviate letter reversal.
Materials needed: scissors and construction paper.

Cut out several letters from construction paper that do not look the same when reversed. (A, H, I, i, l, M, O, o, T, t, U, V, v, W, w, X, x, and Y should not be used.) The small letters *b* and *d* are often troublesome to master correctly as well as *N* and *S*, so these letters would be excellent for this lesson. Throw in a few more that would be helpful for your child. State the letter and hold it up. Is it facing forward or backward? Show the way it ought to look to reinforce the proper form and think of some helpful clues to correctly remember the direction of the lines. Who in the Bible had a view of God's back?

ZANY ZAPPERS

object **lesson**   word **concepts**   nature **science**

Objective: to review the Bible story and word concepts.
Materials needed: several small appliances with electrical cords.

Take a radio, clock, iron, blender, or whatever and face them away from your child with the unplugged cords running toward him. Lightly intertwine the cords, then set the plugs close to your child. Talk about how electricity cannot be seen but must be present in order for the appliances to do their job. Use this as a reminder of the Bible lesson that God is present but unseen. Let your child identify each appliance from the back view. Have him choose a plug and guess what appliance it belongs to. Have him follow the cord with his finger back to its source and see if his guess was correct.

WALKING WITH GOD

physical **activity**   object **lesson**

Objective: to include God as an integral part of life.

Go on a nature walk. Pray and invite God to go with you. Pause and enjoy every bit of wonder. Talk with God as if He were actually present on the walk (as indeed He will be) by thanking Him for each of the beautiful things He made and by taking pleasure in His presence.

WEEK TWO

LOST COIN

story   game

Objective: to present the joy in heaven when God finds a lost person.
Materials needed: a penny.

Hide a penny in a fairly obvious place and let your child look until he finds it. Enjoy the following story of the lost coin, based on Luke 15:8-10. Ask your child if the angels in heaven have ever had a chance to rejoice when he turned from wrong and let God find and keep him. Give an opportunity for response and reaffirmation.

The woman panicked. She laid the coins out on the table top once more. One, two, three, four, five, six, seven, eight, nine. Yes, she was right. One coin was missing and she just had to have it.

Carefully she lit a lamp, holding it up in every dark corner, chasing away the shadows and hoping that along one of the walls she might find the *coin*. Then she grabbed the broom and swept carefully over the entire floor, even sticking the end under the dresser to see if the money had somehow slid underneath. Finally, she emptied every drawer, searched through every pocket, moved every stick of furniture, and poured out the contents of every pot and jar in hopes that somehow, somewhere she would find the coin that was lost.

At last, when she was almost out of ideas, something shiny caught her eye. Was it just the sunshine streaming through the window and playing with the shadow of leaves on the floor? No. There was something caught in the crack between the boards. It was her coin!

She was so happy that she ran to her neighbors and friends, practically dancing with delight. "Be joyful with me!" she shouted in glee. "I have found the coin that I lost!"

In the same way, the angels in heaven are happy when even one person turns away from doing wrong and comes to God.

MATCHING MONEY

Objective: to familiarize your child with currency and give a rudimentary lesson on its worth.

Materials needed: the activity sheet (p. 163) and appropriate coins and paper money.

Lay enough money on the table to match each coin on the activity sheet. Make sure you display one front and one back of the required coins. Let your child match the money by placing the real currency in the right spots on the page. Take him a step further in his knowledge. Can he name each coin? Can he tell how much each is worth? Does he know what combinations equal what? How do we use money? Why did the woman panic when she lost one coin? How would God feel to lose even one person?

MISSING PIECES

Objective: to show the difference between *lost* and *found*.

Materials needed: a puzzle.

Previous to the lesson, hide one of the puzzle pieces in your wallet. Work on the puzzle project together until you complete all but the missing piece. Remind your child of the woman who had all but one of her coins. Where would be a good place to store or keep money? Use that as the first clue in helping your child find the missing puzzle piece. Specify the difference between *lost* and *found*.

CHECKING ACCOUNT

Objective: to practice writing letters and numbers.

Materials needed: slips of paper and a pen.

Copy the approximate formation of your personal checks onto slips of paper for your child to use as an imaginary source of money. Show him where to write the amount he wants to spend, the date, and his signature. Let him write the letters and numbers in the right places. Let him exchange a check for something he would like to purchase: an apple, a story, a hug, or a swing from your hands around in a circle.

BIBLE CHARACTERS

Objective: to ingrain the Bible story in the heart of your child and share a message with those who are lost.

Materials needed: ten coins, a broom, a candle, a bathrobe, and a towel.

This is an excellent story to dramatize. Lay out nine coins on a low table and hide one where your child can see it. Dress him up in typical Israeli garb with robe and headdress. Narrate the story as he acts it out: count the coins, discover the missing currency, look around in frantic alarm, hold up a candle in the corners (unlit, of course), meticulously sweep the floor, discover the missing money, dance in joy, and run out to tell the neighbors. Invite friends and family to watch the reenactment. Make an application to salvation at the end. This is a wonderful chance to help your child share his faith.

WEEK THREE

HOSANNA

story   drama   lesson   activity

Objective: to understand the special joy that comes from praising God.
Materials needed: jackets and tree branches.

Recite the following story found in Luke 19 to your child. When you get to the part about waving palm branches, let your child wave his. When you tell about placing the coats in the road, make a path out of your own jackets. Become a participant in praise.

"Hosanna!" the people shouted. "Praise Him! Jesus is King!" Oh what joy was on their faces as the crowd welcomed Jesus to Jerusalem.

Many of the people that were lining the street and watching for Jesus to pass by had cut palm branches from the nearby trees. They were waving them back and forth above their heads. Others had taken off their coats and were placing them in the street so that the colt that Jesus rode would not even have to dirty his hooves. The clothes that were laid on the ground made a colorful path for Jesus as He rode. He watched the happy, smiling faces of the people as they sang and shouted praises to God.

What a glorious moment! But even then, some of the evil men in the crowd scowled. They did not want Jesus to be the King. They refused to believe He was God. "Tell the people to stop all this fuss," they shouted angrily at Jesus. "Don't let them carry on foolishly like this!"

But Jesus knew that there is always great happiness when people honor God. Jesus knew that he really deserved every bit of praise and glory. So He simply stated a fact when He turned to the evil men and said, "If the people were quiet, the rocks themselves would have to shout out God's praise!"

CARD COLLAGE

arts/crafts   our world

Objective: to remember the Bible story and review the holidays.
Materials needed: old cards from various holidays, scissors, glue, and a light piece of cardboard.

Hunt up and enjoy cards you have saved from birthdays, Christmas, Easter, Valentine's Day, etc. Talk about each holiday and what you traditionally do to celebrate. What holiday came from the Bible story of the Triumphal Entry? Let your child cut out the pictures on the front of the cards to use as the basis for a holiday collage. Glue the pictures onto cardboard.

DOMINO RELAY

word concepts   skill   physical activity

Objective: to discuss the meaning of *before* and *behind*.
Materials needed: dominoes or small narrow blocks.

What did the people do who were walking *before* the Lord? What did the bad people say *behind* Him, after He had passed? Set up a domino relay. As you put one block after another in a line, use the words *behind* and *before* as liberally as possible. When the course is set, push the domino at the end and watch them all fall down.

INVISIBLE INK

pre-reading   arts/crafts   word concepts

Objective: to emphasize the words before and behind and to write letters forming words.

Materials needed: a white crayon, paints, and white paper.

Instruct your child to write with the crayon on the paper one letter at a time as you direct. For example, tell him to draw an *O*. Then have him put a *D* before the *O* and a *G* behind the *O*. Looking at the page before him, he should see nothing since the white crayon is on a white background. Bring the invisible word (*dog*) to light by washing over the paper with a bright coat of paint. Sound out the word. Do this several times with different words.

PRAISE PARTY

Objective: to experience the joy of the Lord and to invent a special holiday.
Materials needed: party stuff of your own choosing.

Make your own holy day to the Lord by planning a "party of praise." Blow up balloons, make confetti, or bake a special treat. Direct your joy and thanks to God for his goodness and kindness just as the crowd that lined the streets did as Jesus entered Jerusalem.

W E E K   F O U R

PLUCKED POSY

Objective: to enforce the concept that joy must be shared.
Materials needed: a flower (real or artificial).

Use the flower as a visual aid while presenting the following story of a flower that wanted to give her joy away. What are some of the ways your child can share the joy that

he has in the Lord with sad and lonely people everywhere? Remember the worth of a simple greeting or a smile.

The little purple flower swayed in the wind. It was a lovely day. She glowed with the pleasure of being alive. Unfurling the last of her delicate petals, she beamed back at the sun.

There was only one small problem that kept her from being perfectly happy. At first, she couldn't actually figure out what it was. It was just a nagging feeling in the back of her mind. But finally after thinking on it awhile, it dawned on her what was wrong. It was not fun to be happy if she could not share it with anybody else. Joy was meant to be spread around.

She was set in the back corner of a huge garden of flowers. So many different colors were placed along the walkways—big, beautiful blooms that could be admired by anyone passing by. But here she was, stuck back behind a large bush. She really felt quite lonely.

Every day for a week she stood up straight and tall. She spread her petals becomingly and tried to smile even at the bees. But it was getting harder and harder to stay happy. Finally, one day a ball came soaring through the air and rolled right up to the little purple blossom. The ball stopped with a bump. Within seconds, a small child followed. He pattered around the big bush to get the ball. As he reached down to retrieve it, a big smile divided his chubby cheeks. "Oh, how pretty," he said. He grabbed the little flower and broke her at the stem. But she didn't mind. At last she could share her joy. The child carried her over to his mother who sat in a chair under the share of a great tree.

"How lovely!" the mother exclaimed as the child handed it to her. "I didn't know we had any flowers as pretty as this." She gently placed the purple posy in a vase with lots of cool water, and the flower thought that her joy could never be greater. She would only be alive for a few more days, but during that time, her happiness could be shared with everyone who passed by her.

TERRARIUM

science   world   crafts   activity

Objective: to appreciate and enjoy plant life first-hand.

Materials needed: a large jar with a lid, soil, rocks, bark, and a small indoor plant or two.

Make a terrarium by arranging the plants, rocks, and bark in soil placed at the bottom of the jar. Water lightly and shut the lid. Place in indirect sunlight. The plant should not have to be watered again for a long time as it creates its own natural environment in the jar. Talk about the story of the flower that wanted to be picked. What does a plant need to live? Does your terrarium provide all the natural ingredients?

IS IT ALIVE?

concepts   science   world

Objective: to determine what is *alive* and what is *not alive*.

Materials needed: scissors and the activity sheet (p. 165).

Cut the page into individual squares. Present each illustration one at a time. Is the item pictured *alive* or *not alive*? Talk about

whether it eats, breathes, or grows. Are flowers, like the one in the story, alive or not alive? Are they able to talk?

DECIDUOUS BRANCHES

science   math   activity

Objective: to give opportunity to count and to provide discussion material on dormancy.

Look for a branch on a tree or bush that still retains some of its leaves. Count the leaves that remain. Where are the rest? What is happening to the tree? Is it still alive? What will it look like next spring? Does every season have its special joys?

WOODLAND RUBBINGS

crafts   world   science   activity

Objective: to develop an appreciation for shapes and patterns found in nature.

Materials needed: a bag, nature specimens, paper, and crayons.

Take an invigorating walk and collect samples of the season: leaves, pods, dried moss, etc. Talk about the joy that the little flower wanted to share. Delight in the loveliness that nature shares at this time of year. Bring the samples home in a bag. Place each under a piece of heavy paper and make a "nature rubbing" by pressing a crayon sideways back and forth across the top of the sheet.

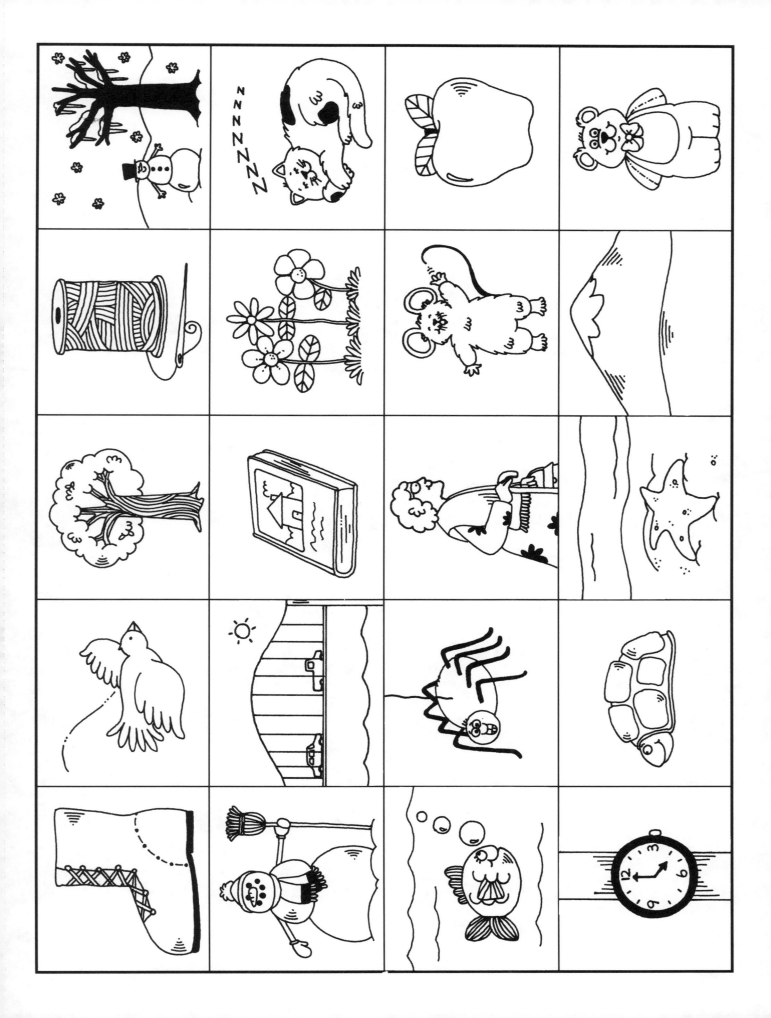

NOVEMBER
WEEK ONE

OUR HOME IN HEAVEN

Objective: to present a time and place when there are no limitations on joy.
Materials needed: the activity sheet (p. 173).

Use the illustrations as a basis for a discussion on heaven. Present our eternal dwelling place as the ultimate fulfillment of all our wishes and hopes. Implant a desire to be there more than anyplace else.

FUTURE FEARS

Objective: to help your child to look toward the future with joy.

Teach your child the right perspective concerning his fears about what the future may hold. Learn Psalm 56:3 together with the accompanying hand motions.

When I /	am a- /	fraid, I will
(clap)	(clap)	(hands on cheeks in gesture of fear)
trust /	in /	You.
(clap)	(clap)	(point to heaven)

DOZEN FRUIT

Objective: to count to twelve and encourage anticipation of heaven.
Materials needed: paper and crayons.

Draw the outline of a large tree. Help your child to think of twelve different fruits to draw in its branches. Suggest lemons, apricots, peaches, apples, bananas, plums, oranges, pears, grapefruit, nectarines, pomegranates, and cherries, etc. Talk about the tree in heaven that will be laden with twelve kinds of fruits (Rev. 22:2). What are some other wonderful things that God is preparing for those who love Him?

NO NIGHT THERE

Objective: to contrast the concepts of *dark* and *light*.
Materials needed: as many different light sources as you can find.

Take a look at a flashlight, lantern, candle, lamp, etc. Show how each works, letting your child participate as he is able. Demonstrate their functions in a shadowy room so the contrast between *light* and *dark* is well displayed. Talk about how heaven will not need to be lighted by any artificial sources but will be illuminated by God Himself.

GOD PROVIDES

Objective: to see God's provision for our future needs.
Materials needed: magazine pictures.

Find the following pictures in books or magazines: clothing, birds, food, flowers, and homes. Discuss the following principles taken from Matthew 6:25-34, using the pictures you have selected to illustrate them. Do you need to worry about having enough *clothes* to wear? No, because the Lord clothes the *flowers* more beautifully than any dresses a person could make. Do we need to worry about having enough *food* to eat? No, because the Lord provides for the *birds*, and they don't know anything about farming. Do we have to worry about having *somewhere to live?* No, because God is making us a home in heaven that is better than anything we could have down here.

WEEK TWO

REBUILDING THE WALLS

skill

story

object lesson

Objective: to show that there is joy in a job well done.

Work on a project together like raking a yard or cleaning out a drawer. After you have worked hard together, celebrate with a little treat. Tell the following story about the rebuilding of the wall found in Nehemiah 8. Empathize with the people's feelings of elation by thinking about your own delight when the chore you worked on together was finally completed.

Nehemiah straightened his back and wiped his brow. He had been working hard. So had all the other people. They were repairing the walls of Jerusalem. Brick by brick, stone by stone, they were replacing the broken sections and sticking them together with clay-like mortar.

It was difficult work for everyone. As the last piece was set into place, the people breathed a sigh of relief. It was worth every bit of energy. It felt great to have the job done. Tomorrow would be a holiday!

In the morning, they cleaned up and put on special clothes. After reading the Bible, Nehemiah told them, "Today is the special day. Have fun. Eat a delicious meal. Drink sweet juices. Share your food with the poor and elderly so they can celebrate too. Be joyful for it is God who gave you the strength to fix the wall, and it is He who will give you the strength to do whatever is to come."

What a wonderful time they had!

SHARPENING UP ON SHAPES

our world

paper-work

Objective: to review and match various sized shapes.
Materials needed: scissors and the activity sheet (p. 175).

Talk about the difficulty of fitting bricks of different shapes and sizes back together to remake the wall. Cut out the shapes on the left-hand side of the activity sheet and let your child match them with the configurations on the right-hand side. Can he name the shapes?

SEWING IN CIRCLES

skill

arts/crafts

word concepts

Objective: to emphasize the meaning of *over* and *under*.
Materials needed: a wide-eyed, blunt needle, yarn, and a Styrofoam meat tray.

Show your child how to make his threaded needle go *over*, *under*, and through the tray to make an interesting pattern. Think about how Nehemiah's men would need to understand instructions like over and under when they were stacking the bricks for the wall.

BALLOON A, B, C'S

pre-reading

word concepts

game

physical activity

Objective: to identify alphabetical letters and reinforce the concept words.
Materials needed: a balloon and an indelible marker.

Before the lesson, write a number of alphabetical letters on a blown-up balloon. Deflate without popping and the letters will shrink to an almost illegible size. Show your child the microscopic alphabet, then let him watch the letters expand as you blow up the balloon. Tie the end. What are the letters and their sounds? Hit the balloon up and around the room. Is the child over the balloon or under? Is the balloon over the child or under?

CARDBOARD CONSTRUCTION

drama   physical activity

Objective: to remember the story from Nehemiah 8.
Materials needed: cardboard boxes.

Beg and borrow cardboard boxes from friends and neighbors to stack and erect a giant wall tower. See how high you can make it and what structures you can construct. Review the story of Nehemiah and the wall.

WEEK THREE

U.S. HISTORY

story   pre-reading   pre-math

Objective: to see how grateful our founding fathers were to be able to establish this land for freedom.
Materials needed: the activity sheet (p. 177).

Read the cartoon with the brief outline of our country's history. Sing "America," learn a line or two of the pledge, or draw an American flag. Pass on a little patriotism.

PILGRIMS

drama   arts/crafts   physical activity

Objective: to establish thanksgiving as a habit, not just a holiday.
Materials needed: construction paper, scissors, markers, and a paper doily.

Be inventive in making a bit of costume flavor to allow your child to step into the life of a Pilgrim. Cut out big yellow buckles to put on his shoes. Make white collars, and wide cuffs to put over his shirt. The girls can use a paper doily for a hat. Talk about the hardships the Pilgrims experienced on their trip in the *Mayflower* and their first year in the new land. How grateful they were for God's assistance and protection in their lives. Are our lives any easier than theirs?

SEQUENCING

word concepts   story

Objective: to further your child's ability to put events in the right order.

Review the series of events in the historical cartoon. Talk about the importance of order. Pick out a familiar story from your child's life—something that happened on your last vacation, the first time he rode a bike, or what it was like when a brother or sister was born. Tell the events of the narration in a mixed-up order. Let your child correct your mistakes. Let him retell the story as it ought to be told.

BOOK LABELS

pre-reading   paper-work   physical activity

Objective: to give opportunity for your child to write his name.
Materials needed: scissors, pen, and the activity sheet (p. 179).

Look over the labels. Discuss the significance of each symbol. Let your child write his name as neatly as he can and choose some of his books to mark with his own identification.

CORN BREAD

skill   pre-math   activity

Objective: to make a recipe that might have been used on the first Thanksgiving.

Materials needed: 1 cup yellow corn meal, 1 cup flour, 2 tbs. sugar, 1 tbs. baking powder, 1 tsp. salt, 1/3 cup oil, 1 egg, 1 cup milk.

Combine the dry ingredients. Mix together the wet ingredients. Stir wet and dry together until just blended. Pour into a buttered 8" square pan. Bake in a preheated 400° oven for twenty-five minutes. Talk about all the things for which you can be thankful.

WEEK FOUR

NOT SO SIMPLE SIMON

story   object lesson   physical activity

Objective: to show that contentment brings joy.
Materials needed: a coin.

Make a quarter disappear by sliding it up your sleeve and "finding" it behind the ear of your child. It's OK if you accidentally muff the trick because you want to explain to your child how the trick is done anyway. Emphasize that there is no real magic involved. After this demonstration, go right into the story of a man named Simon in Acts 8. As long as we are discontent and wishing for things, can we know true joy?

Simon was a magician. He could do many different tricks that would amaze and astonish the people of his city. They thought he was a man with great power. But really he was fooling them by making things seem different than they really were.

Once a man came to his city and preached about Jesus. Simon listened carefully and believed what he said about God. Simon turned away from all the lies he had been telling the people and the evil tricks he used to do and became a believer. He no longer pretended to be a great magician. He served the Lord. He was filled with joy.

Soon Peter and John came to town. They had been friends with Jesus when He was alive on earth. Peter and John did many miracles that showed the people marvelous signs of God's great power. Simon could not believe his eyes. These were not little tricks, meant to fool the people. These were real miracles.

Simon began to think about how fun it used to be when everyone believed he was a great man with super powers. He began to wish he could do amazing miracles like Peter and John. No longer was he happy in Jesus. The more he thought about what he wanted, the more dissatisfied he became.

Finally, he spoke to Jesus' friends. He told them of his wishes for success. He even put his hand in his pocket and offered them a lot of money if they would just tell him the secret of their great powers. "May your money die with you," Peter declared. "God cannot be bought! Your heart is not right before Him. You are wishing for something that is not yours to have now. Pray to God that He may forgive you."

Simon knew that what Peter said was right. It is not good to wish for what you do not have. It did not make him happy at all.

I WISH I HAD....

word concepts   arts/crafts   drama   physical activity

Objective: to differentiate between *bright* and *dull* and between a want and a need.
Materials needed: a drinking straw, cardboard, masking tape, aluminum foil, and scissors.

Construct together a magic wand by using the straw as a stick. Cut out a small cardboard star and tape it to one end of the straw.

Cover the star with foil. What part of the wand is *bright* and what part is *dull*? Pretend your child can use the wand to wish for anything in the world. As he dreams and imagines about his most cherished desires, clarify the difference between a want and a need. Does your child really have to have all those things to make him happy?

J. O. Y.

Objective: to remember that joy does not accompany a multitude of possessions, but acts of unselfishness.

Learn the following poem together. Make body letters by forming the shapes with your arms and legs. When you talk about the letter *J*, extend one arm straight up and curve the other out. To form the letter *O*, put your arms together in a circle over your head. To make a *Y*, place your legs together and slant your arms in a *V* over your head.

> There is only one way to spell joy.
> It is up to each girl and each boy.
> J stands for Jesus, it is there we begin.
> O is for others, make them second to win.
> Y stands for you, behind the first two.
> This is the order for joy that is true.

DISCIPLINE

Objective: to see that we would be very unhappy if allowed to grow up uncorrected.
Materials needed: tree or shrub and pruning shears.

Think about the story of Simon and how Peter had to scold him and warn him of impending punishment if he did not change his ways. Ask your child if he likes to be corrected. Why does a mom or dad have to do it? Bundle up, go outside, and show your child firsthand how to prune a bush or tree. Trim away dead or excess branches to clear the way for new and desired growth. Draw the parallel that although punishments may seem unpleasant at the time, they prune away extra and unneeded behavior. Now your child can grow up to be a stronger and better person.

CONTRASTS OF TONE

Objective: to visualize bright and dull.
Materials needed: four brightly colored crayons and four dull ones.

Help your child to find eight different things that authentically match the color of the crayons that you have selected. Draw them. Have him state which ones are bright and which ones are dull. Is there any practical reason for them to be the color they are?

no more sin

our home

no more pain

God's home

no more death

lots of light

no more tears

lots of beauty

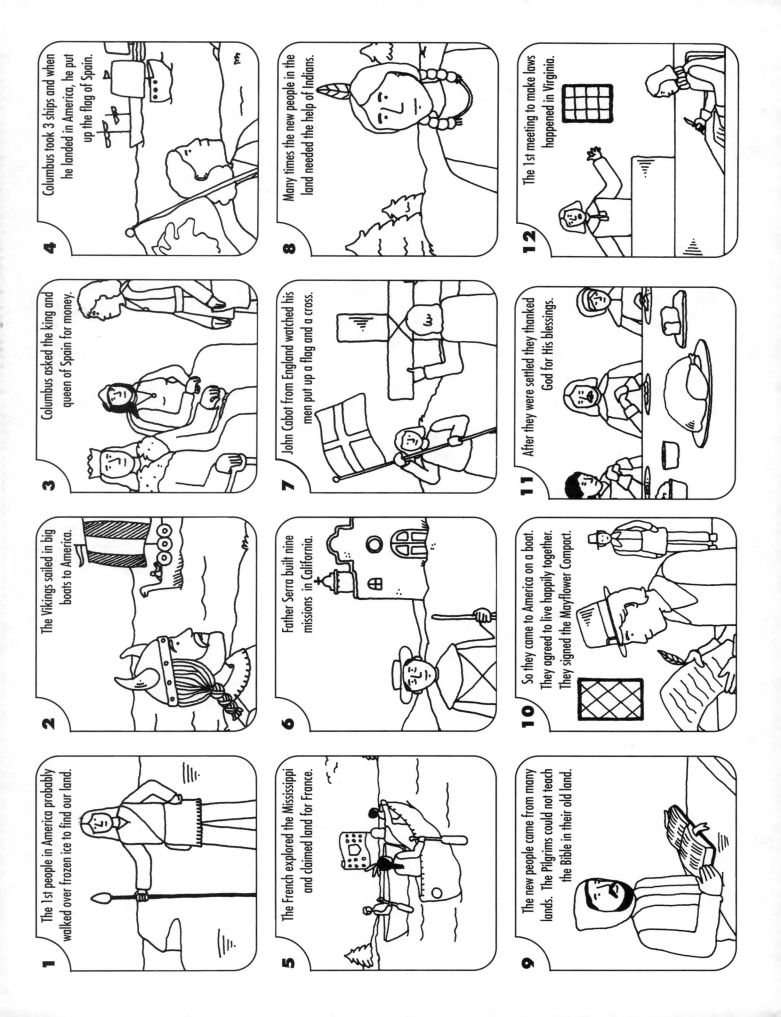

4 Columbus took 3 ships and when he landed in America, he put up the flag of Spain.

8 Many times the new people in the land needed the help of Indians.

12 The 1st meeting to make laws happened in Virginia.

3 Columbus asked the king and queen of Spain for money.

7 John Cabot from England watched his men put up a flag and a cross.

11 After they were settled they thanked God for His blessings.

2 The Vikings sailed in big boats to America.

6 Father Serra built nine missions in California.

10 So they came to America on a boat. They agreed to live happily together. They signed the Mayflower Compact.

1 The 1st people in America probably walked over frozen ice to find our land.

5 The French explored the Mississippi and claimed land for France.

9 The new people came from many lands. The Pilgrims could not teach the Bible in their old land.

This book
belongs to

This book
belongs to

This
book
belongs to

This book
belongs to

This book
belongs to

This
book
belongs to

INDEX